B Goulder

BOAT ENGINES

BOAT ENGINES

A Manual for Work and Pleasure Boats

P. J. BOWYER

David & Charles
Newton Abbot   London   North Pomfret (Vt)

British Library of Cataloguing in Publication Data
Bowyer, Peter J
  Boat engines.
  1. Marine engines. 2. Boats and boating –
  Equipment and supplies
  I. Title
  623.85   VM731

  ISBN 0–7153–7776–0

Typeset by Trade Linotype Limited, Birmingham
          and printed in Great Britain
by Redwood Burn Limited, Trowbridge and Esher
    for David & Charles (Publishers) Limited
    Brunel House Newton Abbot Devon

   Published in the United States of America
          by David & Charles Inc
   North Pomfret Vermont 05053 USA

CONTENTS

PREFACE

One of the most difficult things when writing a book on a subject such as this is deciding the level of technical complexity—especially when aiming to interest a wide range of readers. There is a risk of boring some by oversimplification and going over the heads of others. I have endeavoured to steer a middle course (as appropriate to a book on boats, be they for work or pleasure) by keeping to a semi-technical basis.

Although the reader will note a fair amount of reference to the basics of diesel engines, I have deliberately refrained from writing too much on petrol engines. Not that I have any deep aversion to the subject, but rather that most of us are involved with a car and its petrol engine (sometimes more than we may wish to be), and have acquired a familiarity of sorts with the mechanics of it. Apart from four-stroke car engines, many of us have also received grounding in the two-stroke lawnmower engine—perhaps as a crash course on Sunday afternoon with half of the lawn still to cut!

While on the subject of omissions (no, not *emissions*—these are included) the outboard motor must be mentioned. Although the very large and heavy variety can scarcely be described as portable power units, the simplicity and usefulness of the small motors cannot be denied, and their presence on the boating scene—particularly for inshore pleasure craft —must surely continue as long as suitable fuel is available. However, this is a book on *inboard* engines for pleasure and working boats, which is in itself a broad subject, so that I have avoided any misunderstandings about what may or may not apply to the outboard by leaving this alone.

7

Drawings and diagrams, except where acknowledged, were prepared by my son John and myself with the help of my publishers whose draughtsman, Vic Welch, redrew a number of them.

I have used 'petrol' with reference to fuel and trust that American readers will appreciate that this is the British term for 'gasoline'.

INTRODUCTION

The recent economic climate has not dulled the interest and enthusiasm of the less affluent yachtsman nor killed off the aspirations of would-be boatowners, but higher costs have resulted in an increase both in do-it-yourself activity, and in smaller craft and shared ownership. The 'used' boat market and holiday chartering firms also owe some of their increasing turnover to the high cost of new boats.

For many people, installing an engine in a boat they have built or finished off without professional assistance is the way of graduating from owning a small dinghy or outboard-powered runabout to a boat they can cruise in and live aboard for weekends and holidays. Professionally built craft are becoming increasingly beyond the means of the average family man.

The boating industry is catering for the increasing number of amateur boatbuilders with a wide range of moulded glass-fibre hulls and superstructures for home construction of cruisers and sailing craft. The more ambitious are building their own hull and installing the engine. These days there are many materials and building methods to choose from. As well as the ubiquitous glass fibre, plywood, ferrocement, foam-sandwich construction, steel, aluminium and traditional wood planking have their devotees. Alas, occasionally someone bites off more than he can chew and produces a welded-steel or concrete monument that never gets to the slipway.

However, the majority find that the result of their labours bears some resemblance to the plans, actually floats and requires something to propel it. Hence this book, which is intended to help the builder to understand the principles of propulsion—whether he wants to install the engine himself, or merely to understand enough about the subject so that he can discuss specifications and choose the most suitable model for his purpose. Whether he converted the engine with a marinization kit or bought it, how to carry out the installation and choose suitable ancillary equipment (including the propeller) is dealt with in some detail.

The really keen DIY enthusiast may be tempted to buy a secondhand car engine and marinize it without a kit. It has been done successfully, but it is not easy and requires access to a good workshop to produce the special parts needed. Some of these have to be purchased from specialist suppliers as items such as the water-jacketed exhaust manifold and water pumps, for example, are beyond the capabilities of most amateur mechanics. Chapter 3 gives practical advice to the 'go-it-alone' marinizer.

Because this book is not just for the home boatbuilder or 'do-it-yourselfer', the chapters on powering, marine engine design, installation and propellers are intended for the purchaser of professionally built craft—workboats and pleasure — as well as for boatbuilders who do not specialize in engine installations.

The general aim is to be practical and informative without becoming too technical. Formulae given for calculation of boat speed, for example, are mainly empirical but they have been found useful as a general guide. As regards boat performance, the designer will possess accurate data from trials results, and if he says the maximum speed will be 15 knots with 100 horsepower, while the formula or charts indicate 17 knots at the same displacement, obviously the designer's figure must be used.

I have arranged the chapters in a logical sequence as follows: assessment of the power required, description of the variations in engine design, the choice between buying a complete power unit or marinizing, the installation and selection of the propeller, running boat trials, pollution of the marine environment, and finally, engines of the future.

In the chapter on propellers I emphasize the importance of getting a good 'match' between engine power, shaft speed, and the hull characteristics, so that economical and efficient use is made of the 'energy' used. Too many boats have been fitted with a screw that 'looked about right'.

Observant readers will note that although reference is made to metric units of measurement, in the main imperial units are quoted. Although there is a brave attempt in the engine business to express engine power in kilowatts instead of brake horsepower, and fuel consumption in litres rather than gallons per hour, the more difficult units such as Newton–metres instead of pounds–feet for torque are still being resisted, and engine builders have mainly resorted to dual scales on their power curves. Propeller and sterngear manufacturers are still using inches, but are worried about the time when they will have to use shafts of 25 millimetres instead of 1 inch (25.4 millimetres). This introduces the subject of 'soft' metrication, SI units and other attempts to get the marine-power industry to standardize.

Although reference is made to specific models, information on currently available engines and marinization kits is not included because power ratings and other details change frequently and a collection of manufacturers' literature and price lists is easily obtained.

Regular visitors to boat shows and fishery exhibitions, etc, may have the impression that inboard diesel and petrol engine designs have not changed much in the last fifteen years or so. This is largely true—boatbuilders, marine-engine makers and their customers insist that innovations must be thoroughly tested before expecting people to go to sea with them. However, there have been design changes and there will be many more, particularly now that the prospect of fuel shortages and the effects of the anti-pollution campaigns are being taken seriously by manufacturers as well as legislators throughout the world.

Although this is the age of standardization and rationalization, there are dozens of manufacturers of inboard engines throughout the world, each with a range of power units that incorporate widely varying design concepts. Books can be (and are) written about just one of these engines so that we cannot do a complete analysis of the models and their features in the space available. In dealing with general aspects, therefore, I am using various manufacturers' models to illustrate particular features of engine design and installation practice. Because of the large number of different makes and models, it has not been possible to mention more than a fraction of those available. I must therefore apologize to the many firms who have apparently been ignored, and this includes equipment manufacturers as well as engine builders.

Perhaps the marine-engine business of the future will develop along the lines of the motor-car industry, where most of the smaller firms have disappeared or been incorporated into larger ones, so that although the total number of cars has steadily increased the number of manufacturers has progressively decreased.

Whether this happens or not, in speculation on 'prime movers' for boats of the future, I make the assumption that for the greater part of the power range we are considering, that is, up to about 500bhp, we shall continue to be tied by economic considerations to the automotive type of power unit. This will, in my view, apply to a large percentage of the small craft produced in the future.

In the final chapter I try to answer the question 'What will be powering our cars and trucks, etc, for the rest of this century and the first half of the next, and can we make use of these same power sources to propel the boats of the future?'

1
POWERING THE BOAT

How much power is your boat going to need? Obviously, how big it is and how fast you want to go has a lot to do with it, but it is surprising just how little power in the form of thrust or pull will move a very heavy boat at low speed in smooth water.

A single horse could tow a loaded barge at about 2 miles an hour, but to increase the speed to 4 miles an hour would require several more horses. Incidentally, one horse does not get anywhere near the rate of work which was attributed to the horsepower, that is, 33,000ft lb per min. About two-thirds of this figure is considered a fair estimate of the noble animal's average capabilities.

Like many things to do with boats and engines we can express the power requirement in the form of a graph where pull (or thrust) is plotted against boat speed.

You will see from the graph (Fig 1) that as the boat speed increases, the amount of power required in the form of thrust or pull gets disproportionately greater until it is just not feasible to try to go any faster. In fact, the power would be dissipated in wavemaking resistance, and to go faster would probably swamp the boat. The longer the hull, the faster it can be driven, and so the maximum practical speed can be related to the length. Designers find it convenient to express boat speed (V) in terms of the square root of the hull length (wl) on the waterline, that is, $V = K \sqrt{wl}$. Apart from length, the beam, displacement, hull shape, trim angle, etc, will affect the equation and provide the factor K.

How the resistance curves for different versions of a 25ft boat might look is shown in Fig 2.

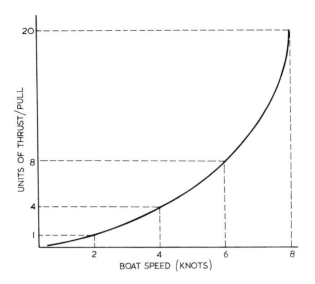

Fig 1   Basic resistance curve

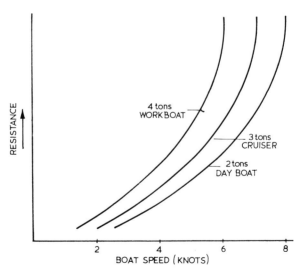

Fig 2   Speed/resistance curves

14

The diagram illustrates the wide variations in resistance offered by different versions of the same length hull. To propel the boat the propeller thrust must overcome hull resistance. The diagram therefore also indicates the wide variations in thrust and hence engine power required to propel a boat according to the type of hull and its displacement, that is, weight (remember Archimedes?)

If you are going to install an engine in a standard hull which can be fitted out in different ways, resulting in differing displacements, the supplier may be able to give you a diagram like Fig 3 that indicates boat speed for varying engine powers at the different levels of displacement that may be achieved. This will have been checked against actual trials results, and provided you can estimate your all-up displacement fairly accurately, you can see precisely what speed a given engine or pair of engines would provide.

If you already have an engine you intend to use you can see from this diagram whether it will do the job or not. An engine which is too powerful but not too heavy or bulky can often be utilized by reducing the maximum operating speed, thereby reducing fuel consumption and noise level, as well as

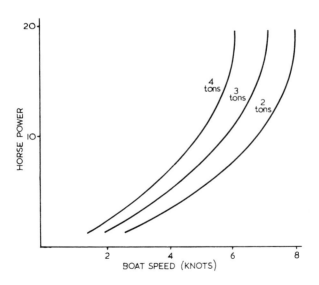

Fig 3   Speed/horsepower curves

15

improving reliability and life. However, it is always advisable to check with the supplier that there are no problems such as vibration periods, which could result from lower-speed running. Engine manufacturers often indicate the operating-speed range on the power curve as shown in Fig 4.

Without the hull builder's speed-power diagram you must use one of the many 'rule-of-thumb' systems for estimating boat speed, which include formulae, charts and special slide rules and nomograms.

Because there are so many variations in hull form which affect resistance, as well as variations in the way the engine power is converted to propulsive thrust, all speed estimating methods are only approximations and should be treated with caution. If the boat achieves 90 per cent of the estimated speed you might just accept this where 10 knots was estimated and 9 achieved. If this is a fast cruiser, however, where 27 knots was obtained but 30 estimated, you might not consider this an acceptable result.

One of the most reliable aids to boat-speed estimation is to

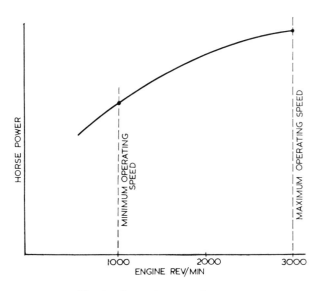

Fig 4 Operating speed range

16

have actual trials data on the same hull—possibly at a different displacement and with a different engine. You can then try out these figures in the speed estimate method you intend to use and make some adjustments if it does not give the right answer so that when you put in your own displacement and engine-power figures you should get an answer that comes close to your trials results.

It goes without saying that the data you use in these calculations must be as accurate as possible—particularly the displacement. Although this can be calculated, by far the most reliable figure is obtained by weighing the boat and then adding the weight of fuel, crew and anything else that was not on board during the weighing.

Different methods are used for speed estimation of displacement and semi-displacement (or semi-planing) craft to the fully planing category.

Engine power is converted to thrust by means of the propeller or jet-propulsion unit. There is no formula for direct conversion of engine power to thrust as this depends on the efficiency of the propulsive system, taking into account losses in bearings, gearboxes or other elements of the transmission.

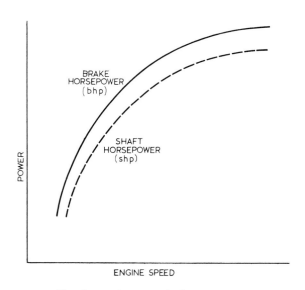

Fig 5   Brake and shaft horsepower

17

Methods of estimating boat speed are usually related to engine shaft horsepower, that is to say, the power available in the propeller shaft, assuming that an average propulsive efficiency is obtainable in the installation. The 'brake horsepower' generally quoted as 'gross' engine power is somewhat higher than the 'shaft' horsepower as indicated in the power curve (Fig 5).

DISPLACEMENT AND SEMI-DISPLACEMENT

Of the several methods available, the simplest to use is a set of curves as given in Fig 6. Some judgement is needed in categorizing the hull form and interpolating between the lines.

ESTIMATING DISPLACEMENT

If you cannot weigh the boat and there is no information available from the hull supplier, the displacement calculation is best left until the boat is in the water, with engine installed and accommodation nearing completion. You need to add to your calculated figure the weight of fuel, water, stores, equipment, passengers, etc not on board, or else add weight in the form of ballast to simulate the total displacement.

So, with the boat in still water and correctly trimmed, mark the position of the waterline at several points around the hull, including the stem and stern (Fig 7). Then, working either from the plan or the actual hull, take measurements of waterline length, maximum waterline beam and maximum draft excluding keel, etc.

We are trying to measure the volume of the immersed section of the hull in cubic feet. If this were a solid block, its volume would be $L \times B \times D$, but a constant, C, has to be brought in to allow for the shape of the hull. This constant varies, of course, according to the underwater shape, and the trick is to get a satisfactory figure or the resulting displacement will be wildly out.

The following coefficients are typical of various hull forms for different types of craft:

Fishing craft and heavy workboats	0.50–0.60
Sturdy cruisers and auxiliary sailing yachts	0.45–0.55
Finer round bilge cruisers and dayboats	0.40–0.45
Hard chine planing craft	0.35–0.40

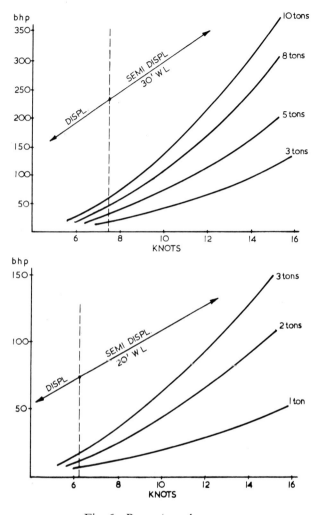

Fig 6 Power/speed curves

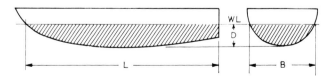

Fig 7 Estimating displacement

19

It is stressed that these are only typical coefficients, and many special hull forms may come outside the values given.

The volume of the hull underwater is $L \times B \times D \times C$ ft³.
The weight of sea water displaced is $\dfrac{L \times B \times D \times C}{35}$ tons.
In fresh water the formula is $\dfrac{L \times B \times D \times C}{36}$ tons.

Many hull designers will quote the block coefficient, and some will supply a table of displacements for various water-line positions. This is a useful piece of data (Fig 8) because with any change in weight caused by taking on extra stores, passengers or fuel, etc, it is easy to check the increased displacement.

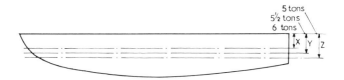

Fig 8   Relating freeboard to displacement

PLANING HULLS

Boats with hull shapes designed to lift and plane when sufficient thrust is applied have a resistance curve similar to that shown in Fig 9. Up to point P the boat behaves like a displacement hull, but increasing thrust takes it through this phase and into the planing condition.

The speed of planing craft (V) is dependent on the hull resistance as well as the displacement, the engine power and the angle of trim (Fig 9).

It may be calculated by the formula $V = K \sqrt{\dfrac{\text{shaft horsepower}}{\text{displacement}}}$

Of course, the constant K is vitally important in getting an accurate speed forecast, and varies widely according to hull type, beam-to-length ratio, skin friction, trim angle, underwater appendages, wind resistance, etc. The values of the constant given below for four types of hull are only typical

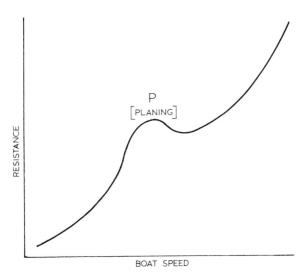

Fig 9   Resistance curve for planing boat

ones and it is advisable to ask the designer for the 'K' value
applying to the hull in question. Certainly you should do this
if the boat has an unconventional hull, such as a cathedral,
catamaran, etc. If you are lucky the hull will have been tank
tested and a graph showing power required for different
speeds against various displacements will be available.

	Typical K values				
Waterline length (ft)	20	25	30	35	40
Old-type, round bottom for'd	2.2	2.4	2.6	2.8	3.0
Narrow vee-bottom design	2.5	2.8	3.0	3.2	3.4
Wide beam, vee-bottom	2.7	2.9	3.2	3.4	3.6
Modern, highly efficient hull	3.0	3.2	3.4	3.7	3.9

If you have any reliable data on your hull, even with a
different all-up displacement and engine power, you can
utilize the equation to obtain K and then use this in your own
calculation. For example, a boat achieves 25 knots with 240
shaft horsepower and 3 tons displacement. Rearranging the
formula,

$$K = \frac{V}{\sqrt[3]{\frac{\text{shaft horsepower}}{\text{displacement}}}} = \frac{25}{\sqrt[3]{\frac{240}{3}}} = 2.8.$$

21

Now that we have estimated how much power will be needed we can decide how to provide it, that is to say, whether single or twin engines will be used, where to locate them in the boat, and the type of transmission system. Of course, you may not be taking things in this order. The engine(s) may already be available—or at least decided on—and the boat may dictate the position of the 'machinery' and type of transmission to drive the propeller(s), or jet drives.

With sailing auxiliaries, the low power required and need to minimize propeller drag, virtually dictates a single propeller shaft. High-powered craft are almost always twin-engined. Medium-speed boats may be single or twin-engined. Small day boats and low-powered craft for inland waterways are usually single-engined as are most working craft—especially fishing boats.

Let us now examine the options available in engine position and power transmission system.

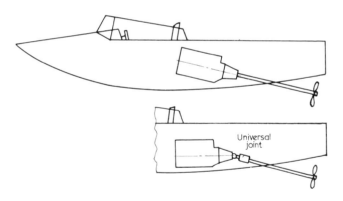

Fig 10   Conventional installation and (*below*) a universal joint
(ie coupling) is shown as an alternative arrangement

CONVENTIONAL INSTALLATION

The engine is positioned more or less amidships (Fig 10), driving the propeller through a reversing gearbox, maybe incorporating reduction gear and directly coupled to the propeller shaft. To keep the engine level and minimize height,

Plate 1 Universal coupling assembly. Note the use of pedestal bearings each side of the twin universal joint assemblies

a universal coupling (or couplings) can be incorporated in the propeller shaft, as shown in Fig 10. Alternatively, a 'down-angle' type of gearbox can be used to maintain a horizontal engine position.

VEE-DRIVES

For many craft, the conventional amidships engine position is inconvenient and prevents the designer achieving a good

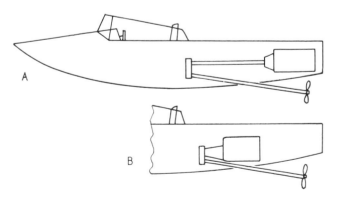

Fig 11   Vee-drives: A – remote-mounted transfer box; B – integral vee-drive

23

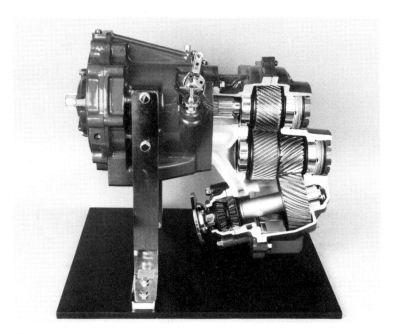

Plate 2 Warner gear Vee-drive, integral with velvet drive transmission
(*Borg Warner*)

accommodation layout. The vee-drive transfer gearbox offers
a solution to this problem, allowing the engine(s) to be
positioned close to the stern and turned around so that the
gearbox end faces forward.

Two different layouts are possible for a vee-drive installation (Fig 11). The transfer gearbox may be an independent
assembly, bolted to extended bearers forward of the engine
and driven by a shaft from the reverse gearbox, which is
fitted to the engine in the conventional manner. Alternatively,
a vee-drive integral with the reverse gearbox may be used. The
engine is usually installed in a near-horizontal plane, while the
propeller shaft is angled to suit the hull requirements.

The engine position close to the stern affects the trim of
the boat and is most suitable for wide-transom, high-speed
craft.

STERNDRIVE

This transmission system becomes more popular each year—

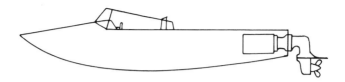

Fig 12 Sterndrive

especially for high-speed pleasure craft—and is gaining acceptance for commercial use in launches, etc, where the maximum amount of space for personnel and gear is required.

The stern-mounted engine is usually attached to the 'through-the-transom' drive unit (Fig 12) so that all of the 'machinery' can be installed with the minimum of alignment problems in the minimum time. Similarly, removal and refitting of engine and drive may be accomplished in a few hours.

The drive unit makes a rudder unnecessary as the assembly

Plate 3 BMW petrol engine with Z-drive, model B220, 3.3 litres (196 cu in), 190bhp (DIN) at 5,500 rev per min (See Fig 13)

25

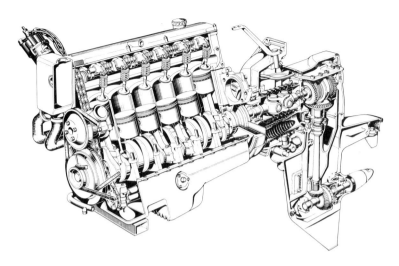

Fig 13   BMW petrol engine, sectional drawing (See Plate 3)

Plate 4 Volvo Penta AQD 21/280 diesel sterndrive

26

Plate 5 Volvo Penta AQ 140/280 petrol sterndrive

is slewed for steering and, to prevent damage when hitting an underwater obstruction, the drive 'kicks-up' like an outboard motor. Further, most drives can be lifted clear of the water for access to the propeller and to provide ground clearance on a mooring which dries out.

Petrol and diesel engines (Fig 13) are used with sterndrives; very heavy diesel engines are not suitable for this arrangement because of weight distribution difficulties in the boat. Apart from 'sterndrive' this system is also referred to as 'inboard/outboard', 'Z-drive' and 'outdrive'.

THROUGH-HULL DRIVE

This is a variation on the sterndrive arrangement, and is particularly suitable for auxiliary-engined sailing craft, because it offers advantages over the conventional engine–gearbox–sterngear layout where space is at a premium in the sailing-boat hull (Fig 15).

The drive unit and engine are usually resiliently mounted to a GRP plinth (Fig 14) which is 'glassed' on the hull, and a rubber diaphragm seals the drive from the ocean. Reverse and reduction gears are contained in the drive assembly, as

27

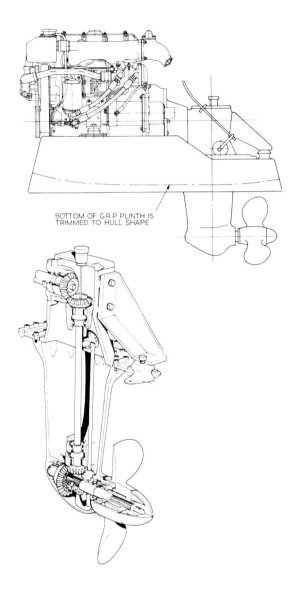

BOTTOM OF G R P PLINTH IS
TRIMMED TO HULL SHAPE

Fig 14   Enfield S-drive fitted to Perkins 4.108 engine:
(*above*) engine and drive assembly; (*below*) section through drive unit
(to different scale)

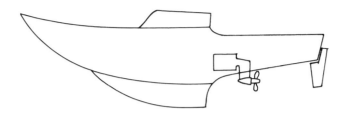

Fig 15   Through-hull drive

with the sterndrive. A reduction in installation time compared
with the conventional arrangement is claimed for this system,
which may be described as an 'S' drive or 'saildrive'.

HYDRAULIC DRIVE

The most compact engine arrangement is possible with this
system (Fig 16) because the engine does not have to be inline
with the propeller shaft. A transverse engine can be fitted and
is often used in hire cruisers where the engine compartment is
aft of the accommodation. Many variations are possible, for
example, several engines each with its hydraulic pump driving

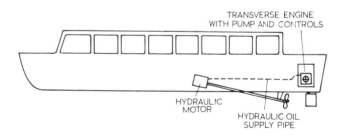

Fig 16   Hydraulic drive (See Plate 8)

a single motor on the propeller shaft. Auxiliary sailing yachts
also find this hydrostatic system convenient because the
hydraulic motor can be located in a narrow section of the
hull with the engine in any convenient (though hopefully
accessible) position.

29

Plate 6 Broads hire cruiser: Reedcraft *Mikado* fitted with ARS hydraulic transmission system

Plate 7 Installation of ARS engine–pump assembly. View through access hatch of hire cruiser forward of transom showing transverse engine

Plate 8 Petter 12bhp engine with ARS pump and hydraulic motor coupled to sterngear with flexible piping (See Fig 16)

JET PROPULSION

Single or multi-stage turbines are coupled direct to the engine which does not require reverse gear because this facility is provided by a deflector plate fitted behind the transom. This arrangement is most popular for sports boats, but is also used for survey craft and other working boats where minimum draft and the absence of propeller and rudder are desirable (Fig 17).

The matching of engine power to the jet power-absorption characteristics is necessary if optimum boat performance is to

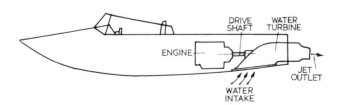

Fig 17   Jet propulsion

31

be obtained. Different turbine diameters and blade shapes, as well as the number of stages, affect the power-absorption characteristics.

The power absorption of three jet units is represented by A, B and C in Fig 18. Model B matches the engine power delivered at rated speed. A will not allow the engine to attain its rated speed, while C is also unsuitable because the engine governor cuts in at rated speed, and only about 70 per cent of the available power will be used in driving the jet unit at point P on the governor run-out curve.

If the engine is an ungoverned petrol engine, the power curve will not cut off sharply at its rated speed, and a match will be attained at Q. However, this entails running continuously at an excessive speed, which may result in a connecting rod passing through the side of the engine (and even the bottom of the boat), so it is not a recommended practice.

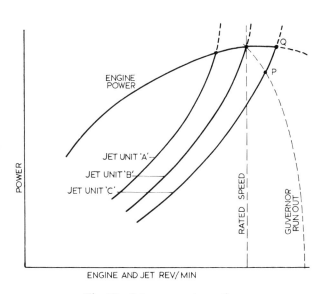

Fig 18   Jet power absorption

ELECTRICAL PROPULSION SYSTEMS

An engine-driven generator supplying current to a motor on the propeller shaft is used on large commercial vessels, but

32

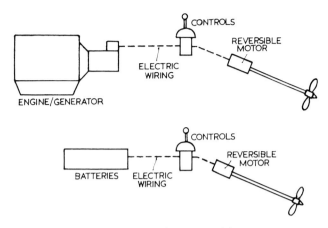

Fig 19   Electrical propulsion

it has not been a popular arrangement for small craft because of the size, weight and cost of the electrical gear required. The principle is similar to that of hydraulic propulsion systems (Fig 19).

Low-powered craft on inland waterways have used lead–acid batteries to supply the propeller shaft motor, but the cost, bulk and limited operating range, coupled with the need to recharge every night, have not made this a popular system.

With the exception of jet propulsion, all the propulsive systems described here terminate in a propeller which develops the thrust to move the boat. Although most of this book is concerned with the means of turning the propeller, the importance of efficiently utilizing the engine power cannot be overstressed, and Chapter 6 is therefore devoted to this subject.

2
ENGINE DESIGN

In this book we are mainly concerned with power units from about 5 to 500 horsepower, although many of the principles dealt with apply to higher-powered engines installed in racing craft, as well as to large engines for commercial vessels.

The term 'boat engines' covers a wide range of pleasure craft from small launches, through many types of dayboat and cruiser, to large auxiliary-engined sailboats where the power requirement is relatively low in comparison to the size of the vessel. The commercial sector embraces scores of different craft, many of which have been developed for a specific purpose, and the only common factor is that, except for barges and pontoons, etc, they all require a means of propulsion.

Engine Types

Present-day inboard boat engines are largely of reciprocating-piston design using petrol or diesel fuel. Many types are available: from one to twelve cylinders, two-stroke or four, naturally aspirated, supercharged or turbocharged, water-cooled or air-cooled, light-weight high-speed or slower-speed heavily built.

As with engines for use on land, the trend in recent years has been towards lighter, faster-revving engines requiring speed reduction gears, and these developments have gone hand-in-hand with new and more efficient boatbuilding techniques and materials, notably glass-reinforced plastics.

The demand for pleasure craft and workboats at reasonable prices, and the increasing production costs of hand-built marine engines, has led to the greater use of automotive–type engines—petrol or diesel—as the basis. Smaller one–, two– and three–cylinder engines are often derived from industrial–type power units produced in large numbers for concrete mixers, electrical generating sets, air compressors, etc. At the top end of the power range marine engines are often evolved from those used to power earthmoving machinery, for example, excavators, bulldozers and scrapers.

Petrol or Diesel?

There has been a steady increase in the use of diesel engines for boats of all types because of the generally superior reliability of the diesel, its better fuel economy and absence of electrical ignition equipment, and the reduced fire risk with diesel fuel.

However, for small boats, particularly on inland waterways where the increased cost of petrol operation is not significant if the boat is only used for about 100 hours per year, the cheaper and lighter petrol engine has its devotees.

In the USA and other countries where petrol is much cheaper than in Europe, high-speed cruisers are fitted with petrol engines up to about 350 horsepower. These engines are lighter than diesel engines of equivalent power, even taking into account the increased weight of the fuel load. Even for these boats, however, the 'diesel option' which is generally offered by the boatbuilder is being increasingly taken up, partly because of the safety aspect, and partly because of the considerable saving in fuel 'energy'.

Workboats of all sizes are rarely fitted with inboard petrol engines nowadays.

Configurations Available

Inline engines from one to eight cylinders, vee-form from two to twelve cylinders, and flat models from two to six are in use although the latter are nowadays less common than formerly (Fig 20). Smoothness improves as the number of cylinders increases. At the same time the necessary weight, or rather the 'inertia', of the flywheel decreases.

Pleasure craft usually have limited space available for the

35

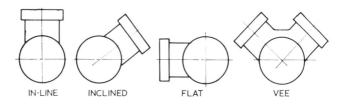

IN-LINE INCLINED FLAT VEE

Fig 20 Engine Configurations

power unit, so that inline engines over six cylinders can seldom be accommodated. V8 models usually make the best use of engine installation space where the power requirements are relatively large.

By far the largest number of boat engines are of four cylinders inline. Good installation practice as described in Chapter 4—particularly in respect of resilient mountings and shaft couplings—will prevent most of the engine vibration being transmitted to the hull, but some of the more lightly built models are difficult to deal with. This problem of 'secondary' harmonic vibrations, that is, occurring at twice the

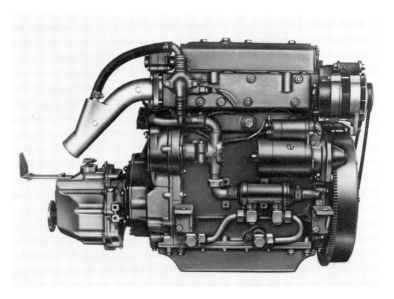

Plate 9 BUKH DV36 ME engine with synchronized balancer, side view (See Fig 21)

36

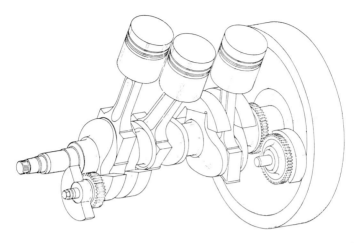

Fig 21 Sectional drawing of a BUKH DV36 ME engine showing arrangement of balancer for 3-cylinder engine (See Plate 9)

firing frequency, was solved many years ago by Lanchester, who fitted a pair of contrarotating counterbalancing shafts below the crankshaft in the sump, running at twice engine speed. This device is currently used in some tractor engines and a few marine models.

BUKH have a synchronized balancer with two counter-rotating weights, gear driven from the crankshaft of their DV36ME engine (Fig 21) as illustrated in Plate 9. This engine is a three-cylinder, inline model.

Practical Examples

Examples of the four different cylinder configurations, with comments on the features and utilization in boats, are given below.

INLINE

This is the most common arrangement, with hundreds of different models, petrol and diesel, produced by scores of manufacturers throughout the world (see Fig 20). Inline engines are generally to be preferred when there is sufficient headroom for installation because the straightforward design simplifies fitting to the boat, and the cost is usually lower than other cylinder configurations.

INCLINED

Inline engines with the cylinders slanted away from the vertical plane to reduce the installation height are useful for pleasure craft where the size of the power unit compartment is restricted or where the engine has to fit under flush decks. Some auxiliary yachts as well as motor cruisers use this type of engine.

Inclined engines are much less common than the vertical inline type. Perkins HT 6.3544 is illustrated in Plate 10. This is a turbocharged diesel engine with the cylinders positioned at 24° above the horizontal.

FLAT

'Flat' engines, in which the cylinder centreline is in the horizontal plane, reduce the engine height to the minimum and are particularly useful as small auxiliary power units for sailing yachts. Flat engines tend to be wide and therefore difficult to install in twin-engined boats where the propeller shaft centres are close together. Plate 11 shows a Farymann

Plate 10 Inclined engine: Perkins HT6.3544

Plate 11 Farymann A40M diesel engine: single cylinder horizontal 12bhp at 2,500 rev per min

Plate 12 Vee-form engine, GM Detroit diesel 8V–71T1 (*General Motors*)

A40M. Horizontally-opposed flat engines with cylinders at 180° to each other are built, but few are available as marine engines at present.

VEE-FORM

These have become more common in recent years, and particularly in the V6 and V8 versions they have the advantage of shortness and moderate width—good features for both pleasure craft and workboats, where smaller engine rooms mean more cargo or passenger space. V4 engines are also produced, although these are much less common than four-cylinder inline models.

The diesel engine illustrated in Plate 12 is a General Motors type 8 V–71T1.

Diesel Engines

As used for the propulsion of boats rather than ships, diesel engines generally develop their maximum power at a governed speed of 1500 rev per min or more, and are classified as 'high speed diesels'.

In general, the smaller the engine the faster it can be made to run. Actually, it is the stroke of the piston which limits the rotational speed, so that short-stroke engines tend to run faster and produce more power from the same cylinder capacity, that is, 'swept volume'. Engines are sometimes built 'over square' where the piston diameter is greater than the stroke in order to run faster. This, of course, applies to petrol as well as diesel engines; both can have a two- or four-stroke operating cycle, which means they have a firing stroke for each revolution or alternate revolutions.

So much for the similarities between petrol and diesel. What are the differences?

Although the modern petrol engine with advanced carburation or petrol injection and a highly developed combustion system and porting will have high efficiency and power potential, the diesel engine will on average have about 50 per cent better thermal efficiency. This advantage comes from a more effective combustion process in which a higher proportion of the heat energy from the fuel is turned into useful work. It is evidenced by the exhaust temperature of a diesel engine being lower than that of a petrol engine.

However, this improved efficiency has to be paid for by heavier weight, increased noise and vibration, plus more sophisticated components. Many of these aspects of diesel engines have been ameliorated by good design practices, some of which are described in the following notes on diesel engine systems and components.

FUEL INJECTION

Injecting very small and accurate amounts of fuel into the cylinders at precisely the right time and at high pressure, also varying the amount and the timing to suit the engine speed and load, is perhaps the most important feature of a diesel

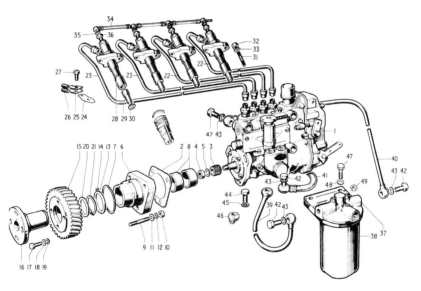

Fig 22   Fuel injection system: Arona AD 495 engine:

1 Injection pump; 2 Gasket; 3 Sleeve; 4 Nut; 5 Washer; 6 Pump bracket; 7 'O' ring; 8 Bushing; 9 Stud; 10 Nut; 11 Washer; 12 Washer; 13 Spacer; 14 Pin; 15 Gear; 16 Hub; 17 Bolt; 18 Washer; 19 Washer; 20 Spacer; 21 Snap ring; 22 Fuel injection pipe; 23 Fuel injection pipe; 24 Brace; 25 Clamp; 26 Sleeve; 27 Capscrew; 28 Nozzle holder; 29 Nozzle; 30 Gasket; 31 Stud; 32 Nut; 33 Washer; 34 Tube; 35 Gasket; 36 Bolt; 37 Fuel filter; 38 Filter element; 39 Fuel tube; 40 Fuel tube; 41 Fuel tube; 42 Bolt; 43 Gasket; 44 Capscrew; 45 Washer; 46 Union; 47 Bolt; 48 Washer; 49 Nut

41

Plate 13 Bosch inline fuel injection pump

engine. The system used in the majority of engines consists of an injection pump, high pressure pipes, injectors and a fuel feed pump with filters. Fig 22 shows the arrangement used on the Arona AD 495 engine.

A Bosch inline fuel pump for multi-cylinder engines is illustrated in Plate 13. A plunger is used for each cylinder, actuated by a camshaft timed to inject fuel before 'top dead centre' on the firing stroke. The stroke of the plungers is fixed, but the rack, which is controlled by the governor, slides in a fore-and-aft direction to rotate the plungers by means of a pinion on each piston, and thus alters the effective size of the outlet ports.

Refinements such as an 'excess fuel' control to assist starting and an advance-and-retard device to vary the injection timing are used. In a distributor-type pump a single pumping element with one, two, or four plungers is employed, with a fuel delivery system similar in effect to the distributor of a petrol engine. A metering valve controls the fuel flow; this is actuated by the governor, which is generally built on to the pump as for an inline model. The CAV DP15 pump is illustrated in Fig 23.

The advance-and-retard device is operated by fuel pressure from the transfer pump. The pumping head is rotated within the body to advance the timing according to the transfer pump pressure. Fuel is injected into the cylinders against the high pressure occurring when the piston approaches the top of its stroke. At 20:1 compression ratio this will be nearly

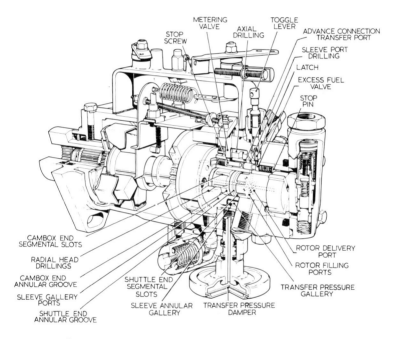

Fig 23 Distributor-type fuel-injection pump, CAV DP 15 model with mechanical governor

900lb per sq in (63 kgf per sq cm). The injector receives each shot of fuel via the high-pressure pipes, the nozzle valve lifts and fuel is sprayed through the small hole or holes in the nozzle (Figs 24, 25), then the valve snaps back on to its seat. This valve is designed to prevent fuel dribbling from the nozzle and to allow the nozzle to 'atomise' the fuel. The assembly is therefore often referred to as an 'atomiser'.

43

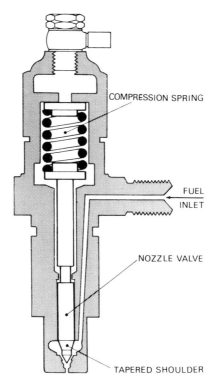

COMPRESSION SPRING

FUEL
INLET

NOZZLE VALVE

TAPERED SHOULDER

Fig 24   CAV pintle-nozzle fuel injector

The pressure setting of the nozzle valve, the size and number of holes, the bore size, and sometimes the length of the high-pressure pipes, contribute to the performance of the fuel-injection equipment and hence do their part in ensuring that the engine will operate economically, smoke-free and giving the power and torque required. 'Over-fuelling', that is, adjusting the fuel injection pump so that it delivers more than the prescribed amount of fuel (which is usually specified in cubic millimetres per 'shot' from the pump) will cause a smoky exhaust and produce very little extra power.

With some engines the fuel pump and injector are combined, a camshaft in the engine operating the pumping element adjacent to the needle valve and injection nozzle. The whole assembly is, of course, located in the cylinder head. A

44

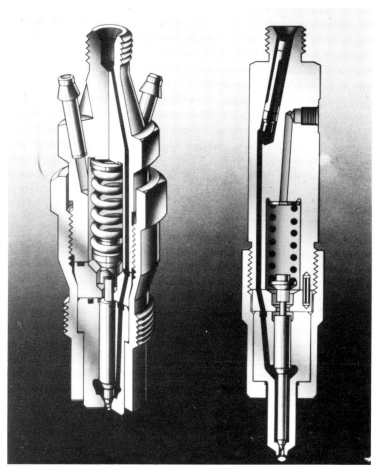

Fig 25   Bosch pintle and multi-hole injectors

sectional drawing of the GM Detroit Diesel arrangement is
shown in Fig 26.

A small amount of fuel leaks from the nozzle valve and
gradually fills the top of the injector body. This is usually
piped back to the fuel tank with the surplus from the fuel
injection pump. The fuel tank in most boats is located below
the level of the engine so that fuel must be 'lifted' to the
injection pump. A fuel lift pump is therefore driven mechanically from the engine, or electrically. The pump illustrated

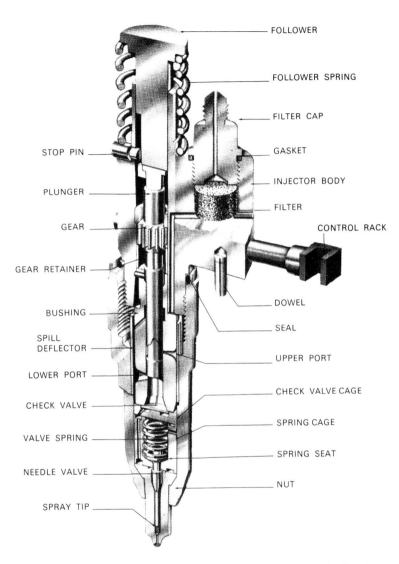

Fig 26 Combined fuel pump and injector, **GM** Detroit diesel

in Fig 27 is a simple diaphragm type by AC Delco.

The last, but by no means the least important, item in the fuel injection equipment is the filter. Paper element types are favoured by most engine manufacturers, and because of the problem of water which is generally present in the fuel, a

46

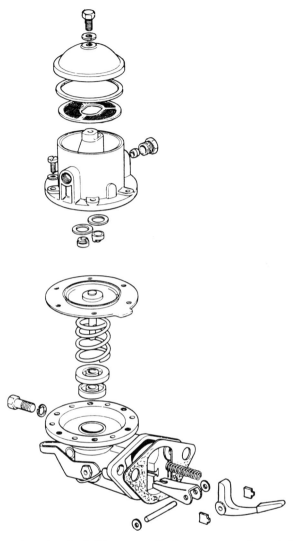

Fig 27 AC Delco fuel lift pump, diaphragm type. Actuated by an eccentric on the engine camshaft (*Perkins*)

filter which separates the drops of water is preferable. Fig 28 shows the CAV 'agglomerator', which would generally be mounted on the engine. A water trap to lose as much water as possible before the fuel reaches the lift pump is recommended to be fitted close to the tank (see Chapter 4).

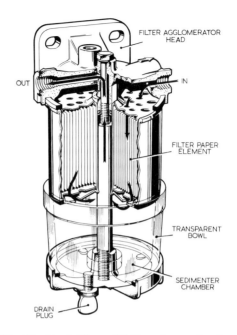

FILTER AGGLOMERATOR HEAD

OUT

IN

FILTER PAPER ELEMENT

TRANSPARENT BOWL

SEDIMENTER CHAMBER

DRAIN PLUG

Fig 28   Fuel filter: CAV agglomerator type

COMBUSTION SYSTEMS

The variety of shapes and sizes of combustion chamber which have been used for diesel and petrol engines is infinite. Designers strive for performance, economy and, in the case of diesel engines, minimal smoke. The mixing of air and fuel is all important so that the design of the inlet and exhaust ports, as well as the combustion area, is arranged to cause phenomena such as 'squish' or 'swirl'. Air movements are measured and filmed on models of the combustion system, and there are computer programs for calculating all aspects of combustion to save some of the 'trial and error' approach.

Diesel engines have two main classifications—'direct' and 'indirect' combustion. With the direct system fuel is sprayed into a combustion bowl formed in the crown of the piston; with indirect combustion there is a separate chamber in the cylinder head. These two basic designs, which include combinations of both arrangements designed to obtain the advant-

48

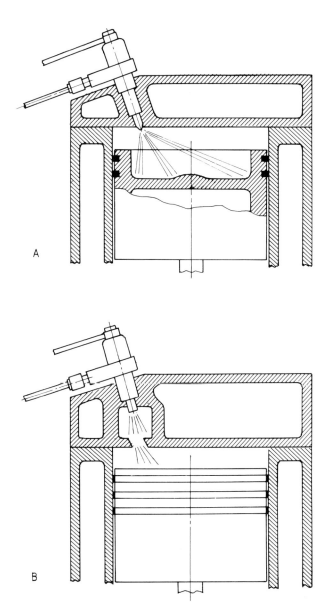

Fig 29 Combustion systems: direct and indirect diesel systems:
A – direct injection with combustion chamber in piston and multi-hole
fuel injector; B – indirect injection with combustion chamber in
    cylinder head, flat topped piston and pintle type fuel injector

ages of each system, are illustrated in Fig 29.

Indirect systems were the first to appear in the early auto-motive-type engines of the 1930s. Engines were able to obtain the higher speeds needed for road transportation. Later development of direct systems showed that easier starting and better fuel economy were possible, although combustion efficiency fell off at the higher speeds. More recent development has resulted in DI engines running at higher speeds with the result that there is no clear demarcation between DI and IDI engines. The smaller, higher-speed type, however, tend to favour the latter system.

DIESEL STARTING AIDS

The temperature at which an engine will start depends upon the following factors:

ambient air temperature,
capability of the starting motor to achieve a minimum cranking speed,
viscosity of lubricating oil,
drag from engine and transmission,
inertia effect of flywheel and engine,
'startability' of engine, and
general condition of engine.

These factors will be taken into account when an engine manufacturer quotes a minimum ambient temperature for starting, and it must be assumed that the important settings, such as fuel pump timing, fuel delivery adjustment of injection pump and valve clearances have not been tampered with. The statement on cold-starting performance would then take the following form:

'Unaided starting for an engine built to specification No .... at temperatures above $-10°C$ (15°F) with SAE 20W lubricating oil and minimum cranking speed 120 rev per min.'

To improve starting temperatures for engines which have a limit of freezing point or above, there are various aids which may be fitted by the engine manufacturer.

Excess Fuel

This arrangement is provided on some fuel injection pumps to 'richen' the air–fuel mixture in a similar manner to the choke used on petrol engines.

Heater Plugs

Possibly the simplest aid for an engine fitted with electrical equipment, a heating element is screwed into the combustion chamber of each cylinder and wired up to a starting switch, so that a period of 'pre-heat' precedes the actual start.

Thermostart

This arrangement is manufactured by CAV and consists of an electrically-heated element which ignites fuel oil to burn in the induction tract and provide heat just prior to starting, and also during, the actual start. The fuel supply is controlled by a bimetallic strip so that fuel is not admitted until this has heated up. Switching off the current cuts off the fuel supply (see Fig 30).

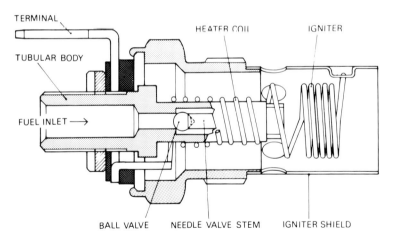

Fig 30   CAV thermostart

Ether Starting

Ether will aid starting even at very low temperatures, but it must be administered correctly. If used in excess, very high pressure could build up in the cylinder and result in engine damage. It is preferable to use a nozzle fitted in the induction manifold, with a feed system approved by the engine manufacturer, rather than aerosol cans which should be used in an emergency only.

Using ether with heater plugs or Thermostart, etc, is dangerous and could cause an explosion.

When workboats are operated at very low temperatures, say, −30°C (−22°F) or below, it is desirable to keep the oil sump and cylinder water-jackets warm by fitting immersion heaters. It is advisable to plug these into a mains electricity supply if available, because the battery drain coupled with the starter-motor power requirement is likely to be beyond the capacity of all but extremely large batteries. Some form of heating will be required in the engine room if immersion heaters are impracticable.

Starting Systems

HAND STARTING

The human starter is probably the most reliable one as it does not require a charged battery. It does, however, require a fairly good physical condition to turn the engine over. The operator will be able to swing quite large petrol engines equipped with overhead starting gear and diesel engines up to about 30 bhp. Larger diesel engines are rarely fitted with hand-starting equipment. All hand-started engines require decompression gear to allow a good cranking speed to be built up before engaging the lever which causes the valves to seat fully and thus build up compression pressure. Some multi-cylinder engines bring in one cylinder at a time.

ELECTRIC STARTERS

The most common and convenient starting system for boats with electrical equipment is the electric motor with an alternator or DC generator to keep the battery charged. The car-type starter with 'Bendix' drive to the pinion is used for many petrol engines and the smaller diesel models. For larger diesel engines, particularly workboat installations, a solenoid-operated positive engagement and disengagement type of starter is often specified, as this will generally give better

Plate 14 Bosch 'Bendix' drive starter

Plate 15 CAV positive engagement starter

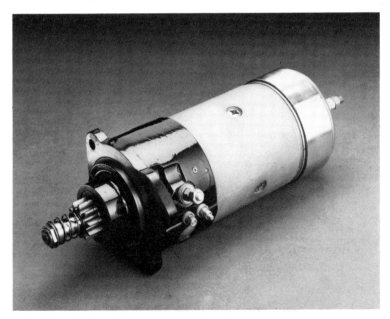

53

service. In cases where starting is difficult at low temperature this type is less likely to slip out of mesh before the engine picks up speed.

IMPULSE STARTERS

Various mechanical starters which store energy by means of a powerful spring or flywheel inertia are available and may be used as an alternative to electrical systems or as a standby to get the engine started if the battery is discharged. The Lucas-CAV spring starter is illustrated in Plate 16. This is cranked by hand to wind up the spring.

Impulse starters generally turn the engine over at high speed for a few revolutions. Some designs allow the engine to be motored over slowly to assist in bleeding air from the fuel system.

HYDRAULIC STARTERS

An hydraulic cranking motor similar in appearance to an electric starter is actuated by oil which is pressurized in an

Plate 16 Lucas–CAV spring starter

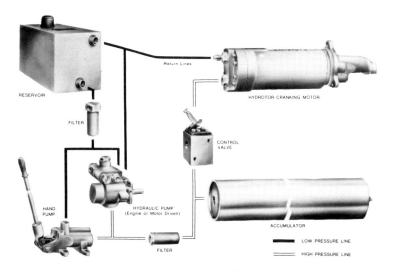

Plate 17 American Bosch hydraulic–cranking system

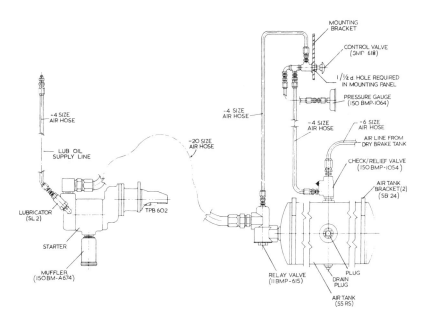

Fig 31 Ingersoll Rand air starter installation

accumulator where air or an inert gas is pumped up by hand or by an engine-driven charging pump. Selection of a suitable hydraulic motor and ancillary equipment enables very good starting performance to be obtained, and once the engine is started for the first time the engine-driven pump will store sufficient energy in the accumulator for the next start.

The system illustrated in Plate 17 is manufactured by American Bosch (Hydrotor).

AIR STARTING

This system is convenient for large propulsion and auxiliary engines used on ships where there is a source of air pressure. On smaller vessels air starting may be employed by providing a reservoir and charging pump similar in principle to the hydraulic system.

An Ingersoll–Rand system is illustrated in Fig 31.

Petrol Engines

Although most of the 'marinizing' features of the marine petrol engine are the same as for the diesel, so that much of Chapter 3 applies to both, there will be differences in the 'basic' part of the engine when this has been designed for sea-going use. As most of these models are based upon car engines, the general configuration will be familiar, except perhaps where American six- and eight-cylinder engines are imported to Europe.

A prime requirement is to combat the effects of dampness on the ignition system, starter motor and alternator, and any other exposed components which are likely to corrode. The carburettor may be of several different types, although basic-ally with either a fixed or variable jet. Here again the need is to resist the corrosive effects of salt-laden sea air without blocking jets or jamming moving parts. It must also operate at varying angles of inclination without unduly affecting fuel flow.

Safety precautions are, of course, vital when petrol is used as the fuel, and various devices are available to detect its presence as a vapour in the bilges. However, it is advisable to use a spark-proof alternator and starter motor, relays, switches, etc.

56

Condensation in the fuel tank is likely to cause frequent problems with sludge in the carburettor unless a water trap or water-separating filter is fitted.

Two features of modern petrol engines are fuel injection by means of a very similar system to the rotary pumps used with diesel engines, and a 'solid-state' ignition system which avoids the need for the mechanical 'make-and-break' arrangement in the distributor. More precise control of fuel and more even distribution to the cylinders are claimed with the former, while the latter gives a more consistent spark at the plug electrodes. These features allow better economy, flexibility, and reliability of operation.

Governing

When the engine is coupled to a propeller its maximum speed will be limited by the propeller—in effect, the engine is governed by the propeller. A properly matched propeller will govern the engine to its rated speed, or a lower speed if so desired (see Fig 32).

In disturbed water the propeller will slip and the engine revs can suddenly fly up to a dangerous speed unless the

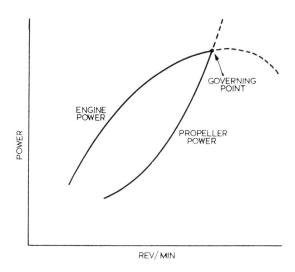

Fig 32   Propeller governing

57

throttle is rapidly closed. A speed governor fitted to the engine will do this automatically by sensing an increase in speed as it starts to occur and immediately taking corrective action. With a fuel-injection pump as fitted to a diesel or petrol injection engine, the governor controls the valve which meters fuel to the injectors. Three governing systems are in use:

1. Mechanical governor, where the centrifugal force from rotating flyweights is coupled by linkage to the fuel metering valve.
2. Hydraulic governor, using fuel pressure within the injection pump as the controlling medium.
3. Electronic governor, monitoring changes in engine speed by an electronic sensor.

Petrol engines installed in boats are not generally fitted with governors. However, a simple speed control governor is available for carburettor engines, working by sensing the velocity of the incoming air and closing the throttle when the limiting velocity is reached.

Alternative Power Units

Piston engines, as applied to boats, have two rivals as far as pleasure craft are concerned.

WANKEL

This rotary engine is in production for cars and as an outboard for power boats. Using low-grade petrol fuel, its compact size and smooth operating characteristics, coupled with present-day improved reliability and fuel consumption, make it a potential rival to the conventional automotive type of petrol engine. Attempts to produce a diesel version have so far been unsuccessful, largely because of rotor sealing problems and an inability to obtain a high compression ratio.

Operation of the engine is as follows:

The three-sided rotor is connected to the crankshaft by an eccentric journal so that it orbits with a geometry which allows the three tips to remain in contact with the trochoidal housing. This forms chambers within the casing which constantly change shape to allow the four phases to be performed within one-third of a complete revolution (see Fig 33). Three power 'strokes' are thus performed for each revolution of the rotor. As well as rotating on the eccentric journal, the rotor is geared to the crankshaft so that there are three crankshaft revolutions for each rotation of the rotor.

The compact form of this engine enables high power to be obtained from a relatively small swept volume. For example,

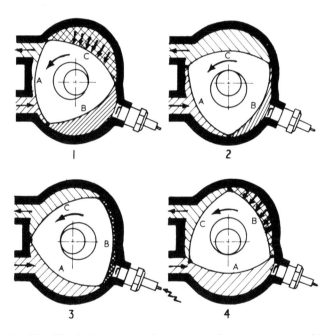

Fig 33 The Wankel rotary engine: 1 induction commences with face A opening the inlet port; B compresses the air-fuel mixture trapped in this segment; C is under pressure from the ignited charge – ie producing power; 2 A has opened more of the induction area; B has almost completed compression of the mixture; C is directing exhaust gases through the outlet port; 3 A continues to induce the air-fuel mixture; B has fully compressed the charge and the spark plug ignites it; C continues the exhaust ejection; 4 A is about to close off the inlet port; B is under pressure from the ignited charge, ie producing power; C has almost completed the scavenging of exhaust gases

35 bhp at 5500 rev per min is obtainable from a 518cc OMC engine (a conventional reciprocating four-cylinder petrol engine would require about 1000cc for the same power output).

The Wankel engine runs smoothly because there is no out-of-balance vibration from the eccentric rotor. However there is a cyclic torque fluctuation characteristic which is improved by increasing the number of rotors.

One of the problems which occurs with many conventional piston engine installations is excessive exhaust back-pressure, but this is particularly important to rotary engines such as the Wankel, and it is very important to keep within the maker's requirements. The engine is also vulnerable to high temperature in the combustion area for the following reasons: there is no cooling effect from the incoming charge on the compression stroke as with a piston engine; because there are three firing strokes per revolution, the exhaust port does not close, and the sparking plug has to work at high temperature. However, the excellent cooling facility available to a water-cooled outboard or inboard engine goes a long way towards overcoming this inbuilt problem, just as the water injection exhaust system and generous pipe sizes can minimize exhaust back-pressure.

GAS TURBINE

Application of the aircraft type to large vessels such as motor torpedo boats has been successful, and has led to racing craft using the same engines. High performance and high power-to-weight ratio are the main advantages; poor fuel economy and high noise level are disadvantages, although many devices have been developed to improve the fuel consumption characteristics. High-output shaft speed necessitates reduction gearing to match the propeller speed. The sophistication, and therefore high cost, of these engines makes them unlikely to become popular for power boats unless they are developed for mass production as road vehicle power units, giving a 'spin-off' to the boating industry. The possibility of this is explored in Chapter 9.

Most of the current gas-turbine engines used for marine propulsion are well above our 500 bhp power ceiling.

The Garrett IE 831–800 model develops 690 continuous

Plate 18 Detroit Diesel Allison gas turbine, model GT 404/505

shp at a variety of output shaft speeds, according to which of
the reduction gear ratios is selected. Two Detroit Diesel
Allison automotive-type gas turbines develop 360 and 460 bhp
(270 and 340 kW) respectively at 2880 rev per min. The latter
model is illustrated in Plate 18.

Power

Whatever the type of engine, its power is generally expressed
as 'brake horsepower' given at the maximum speed. Because
we need to know what power is developed at lower speeds

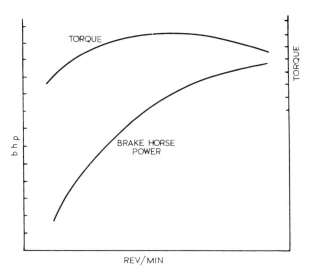

Fig 34　Power and torque curves

also, a power curve is produced from a test run with the engine fitted to a dynamometer recording power over the speed range. The test brake in fact records the torque of the engine, that is, the 'twisting moment' on the shaft (Fig 34), and from the torque curve the bhp curve is derived by using the following formula:

$$\text{brake horsepower} = \frac{\text{torque (lbf ft)} \times \text{engine rev per min}}{5252}$$

Three sets of units are in current use to define torque:

pounds feet	lbf ft
kilogramme metres	kgf m
Newton metres	Nm

Similarly, there are three units for power:

brake horsepower	bhp
kilowatts	kW
Pferdestärke or cheval vapeur	Ps cv (ch)

1 bhp = 0.7457 kW　　　　　1 lbf ft = 0.1383 kgf m
1 bhp = 1.0139 cv　　　　　1 lbf ft = 1.3558 Nm

Engine power is affected by the operating conditions which govern the amount of air delivered to the cylinders. This affects the air–fuel mixture on diesel engines and petrol engines, whether using carburettors or injection pumps. The varying conditions are altitude (rarely of concern to boat engines), atmospheric pressure, percentage humidity and air temperature. Unfortunately, the world has not agreed on a common rating standard so that the SAE, German DIN and British Standards, to quote the principal contenders, are different (Fig 35), and you will see in the small print on the engine maker's power curves the reference conditions to which the particular curve relates. The same power expressed to SAE J270 1.3.4, for example, will appear approximately 3 per cent higher under BS AU 141a:1971 conditions. The total barometer reading and ambient air temperature for the five most common rating standards are tabulated below:

	Total Baro	*Air Temp.*
BS AU 141a: 1971	29.92 in (760 mm)	68°F (20°C)
BS 649: 1958	29.5 in (749 mm)	85°F (29.4°C)
SAE J270 1.3.4.	29.38 in (746 mm)	85°F (29.4°C)
DIN 70020	29.92 in (760 mm)	68°F (20°C)
DIN 6270 A or B	29.0 in (736 mm)	68°F (20°C)

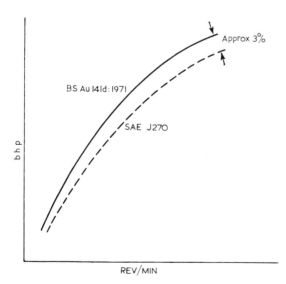

Fig 35   Rating standards

Turbocharging

The power output of petrol and diesel engines is limited by the amount of air that can be induced into the cylinders. There is no difficulty in increasing the amount of fuel, but this has to be accompanied by sufficient air to achieve satisfactory combustion.

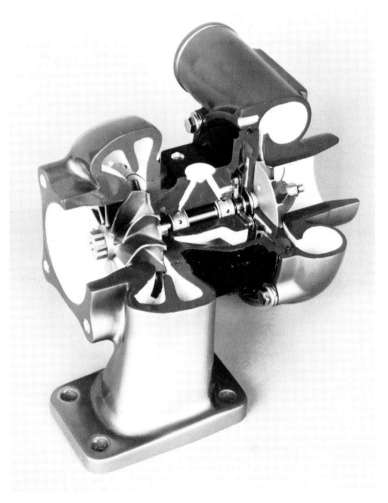

Plate 19 Exhaust driven turbocharger: Holset turbocharger cut–away model showing turbine wheel on left side of shaft and compressor wheel on right

By using the largest possible inlet valves, 'tuning' the induction system, or arranging a ram effect on high-speed boats, the maximum weight of air can be introduced to a naturally aspirated engine. Mechanically driven air pumps of various designs have been used for four-stroke engines to 'supercharge' the cylinders and are still used to scavenge two-stroke units. The most popular system for present-day petrol and diesel engines is an exhaust-gas-driven turbocharger.

The exhaust turbine is driven by the gas stream and achieves speeds of up to about 80,000 rev per min. The energy used is virtually free—there is a slight increase in back-pressure on the engine, but a correctly matched turbocharger will not have any adverse effect on this area.

The compressor which is coupled to the turbine will increase the weight of air to the cylinders by about 50 per cent at maximum engine speed. This percentage is reduced at lower engine speeds because the amount of energy in the exhaust is correspondingly reduced. By increasing the fuel supply to match the improved air flow, the engine power can be considerably increased—about 50 per cent increase is normal for pleasure-craft engines, but over 300 per cent is feasible for short-life racing engines. A typical turbocharged-

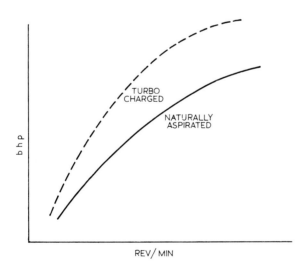

Fig 36   Power boost effect of turbocharging

65

engine power curve compared with its naturally aspirated counterpart is shown in Fig 36. Note that the power at lower speeds is little better than the non-turbocharged version.

Increasing the power of an engine which was not designed for it can have disastrous effects on the engine life and reliability. The cylinder pressure increases considerably; this affects the bearing loads—big ends and mains, lubricating oil and cooling water temperatures, as well as stresses and

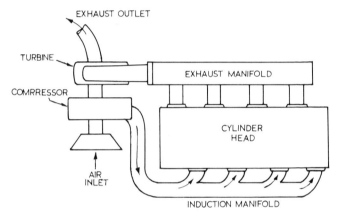

Fig 37A   Turbocharging system (seen from above)

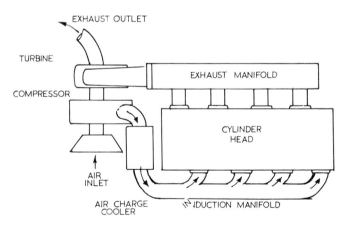

Fig 37B   Turbocharging with charge cooler (seen from above)

vibrations in many engine components. Beware, therefore, of fitting a turbocharger to an engine which was definitely not designed for it!

AIR-CHARGE COOLER

The turbocharger compressor pressurises the air to about 8–15 lbf per sq in (ie boost pressure) and also raises its temperature. By cooling the air before it passes into the cylinders, a greater weight of air can be introduced and the critical temperatures in the piston crown will be reduced with a corresponding improvement in reliability.

Turbocharged boat engines have a considerable advantage over land-based ones because the air-charge cooler (Fig 38) can be cooled by sea water and thus its size is minimized.

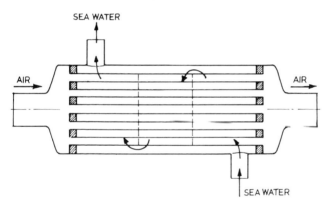

Fig 38   Air-charge cooler (sectional view)

High Performance Engines

PETROL

Outboard motors have dominated the sports boat and racing scene, although offshore power-boat racing has been responsible for the adaptation of Grand Prix racing-car engines and specially tuned inboards and sterndrive power units.

Boosting the output of a car engine by increasing the compression ratio, fitting stronger valve springs, high-lift camshaft, polishing the ports, connecting rods and crankshaft, new manifolds and carburettor has been practised by generations of sports-car enthusiasts, and more recently applied to boat engines.

Turbocharging engines (if racing rules allow) has provided the ultimate in power boosting. It also enables a smaller engine to give the power of a larger one—four-cylinder instead of six, six-cylinder instead of V8. The weight reduction gives increased boat speed.

The life of the super-tuned racing engine may be reduced to about 10–25 hours from the original 1000–2000, so that frequent and expensive rebuilds are required.

DIESEL

With diesels it is a little more difficult to get high outputs without overstressing the crankshaft, bearings, etc, and overheating the pistons and valves. As the power is increased by higher air boost pressure and fuel delivery to match, the maximum cylinder temperature and pressure increase; the compression ratio must be reduced in order to prevent engine damage. A direct-injection engine with compression ratio of, say, $16:1$ has to be reduced to about $12:1$.

Sabre Engines have developed a 365 bhp version of their six-cylinder 363cu in (5.95l) Ford conversion. As 'startability'

Plate 20 Sabre 365 racing engine, 365bhp at 2,400 rev per min

deteriorates when the compression ratio is lowered, Sabre have adopted the use of paraffin (kerosene) for starting with a dual-fuel system to supply diesel oil for normal running.

To improve low-speed torque to get boats up on the plane, oxygen is injected into the cylinders when accelerating.

Engine Heat Utilization

Use can be made of the heat which the engine passes to its cooling system to operate a small space heater or a calorifier to provide hot water for the sink and wash basin. The amount of heat available is limited, and is only worth utilizing if the engine is used for fairly long periods at cruising speed to full speed. It must be fresh-water cooled by heat exchanger—direct-cooled water temperatures are too low and keel-cooled systems are generally difficult to control so that the heat goes through the external heating circuit when required.

It is possible to use a long length of water-jacketed exhaust pipe, providing the engine is run for long periods at full load. In connecting up to the engine you must position the fittings so that a flow is obtained without interfering with the engine cooling circuit. On most engines the flow can be taken from the cylinder-head outlet and returned to the fresh-water pump

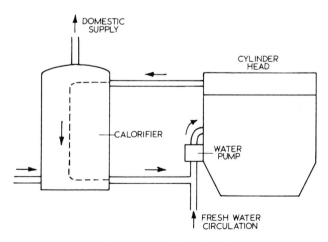

Fig 39   Calorifier   circuit

inlet. The water passes through a coil inside the calorifier like a domestic 'indirect' hot water cylinder (Fig 39) so that your engine cooling circuit does not mix with the domestic supply.

To avoid heat loss keep pipes as short as possible and lag them. Fit air-vent plugs at the top of the system and drain connections at the bottom. Make sure that the system is properly filled to avoid air pockets which will prevent flow through the circuit.

3

MARINIZATION

While Chapter 2 was concerned with the 'basic' design of engines, we now come to that part of the design which has to do with the marine application.

There are three classifications of boat engine:

1 Those designed, developed and built solely for marine use.
2 Engines adapted from industrial, agricultural or automotive types.
3 Models which are 'marinized' versions of industrial, agricultural or automotive engines.

Group 1 is almost entirely comprised of diesel engines. Nowadays, few petrol engines are built specifically for use in boats. Reciprocating ships' engines, of course, come entirely within this group, but in the boat power range the tendency in recent years has been for larger numbers to be produced from groups 2 and 3. Examples of group 1 are Kelvin, Mirlees Blackstone and Arona.

Group 2 allows the financial benefits of large-quantity production of the more expensive engine components, such as cylinder block, cylinder head and crankshaft, to be obtained. Special marine components, that is, the sump, manifolds and corrosion-proofed valve springs, can be introduced into the engine build in place of the automotive-type components. Group 2 mainly consists of diesel engines, and examples of these are Cummins, Perkins and Volvo Penta.

Group 3 covers many makes of marinized engine, both petrol and diesel. Marinized petrol engines are mainly confined to the pleasure craft sector, especially in areas outside North America. Marinized diesels are also largely used for pleasure craft.

Engines for marinization are generally supplied from the manufacturer to a firm specializing in marine conversions and marketing the finished product. As they are fitted with the original sump, manifold, etc, the engine has to be stripped if the automotive-type components are to be replaced. Companies supplying petrol and diesel engines for marinization include Ford, British Leyland and Villiers.

Firms dealing with engines in group 3 can be subdivided into three classes:

1 Companies specializing in engine conversion—fitting transmissions and supplying accessories such as instruments and exhaust systems, as well as arranging the cooling systems, etc. This is a highly skilled undertaking, and considerable ingenuity is often necessary to produce a good design which uses as much of the original engine as possible and does not look like a 'plumber's nightmare'. A large number of firms undertake this work; for example, Tempest Diesels and C-Power (Marine) Ltd convert Ford and British Leyland diesels, while Watermota Ltd offer marinized petrol and diesel models adapted from Ford, Briggs and Stratton, Villiers and Petters base units.

2 Kit manufacturers supplying the necessary components to convert a car or truck engine to marine use. Some of the marinizing companies also supply conversion kits. Others specialize in kits, covering a larger range of engine types than any engine marinizer can handle. Most kit suppliers will also sell separate components, such as water-cooled exhaust manifolds, as replacements and for those people whose engines fall under group 3. Kit suppliers include Lancing Marine, C/T Marine and Wortham Blake.

3 Individual converters of engines. This work is mainly carried out by the do-it-yourselfer who needs to reduce engine costs to the minimum and may confine

Plate 21 Basic conversion kit: from top, left to right: water-cooled manifold, engine mounting frame, cylinder head water outlet, water pump incorporating water pressure switch, oil cooler, oil filter (disposable), water inlet skin fitting, tachometer, ignition solenoid with warning lights under, starter motor mounting with starter solenoid attached, flywheel adaptation plate for Ford flywheels, flexible drive element which couples direct to Transa Drive, adaptor plate for Hamilton Jet Pump and flywheel coupling bar and rubber drive element to connect to Enfield outdrive. To the left is the engine mounting frame with bolts supplied

his boating activities to inland waterways or short coastal passages. Although some conversion parts may be purchased, the majority of components are made up by the marinizer. This may be necessary because the engine being converted is not a model for which kits or components are available.

The Choice

The larger engine manufacturers generally supply boatbuilders via their agents or distributors, who will advise the purchaser on technical as well as commercial questions, and offer a comprehensive choice of specification. The manufacturer backs up his distributors by dealing with the more difficult technical queries.

With a 'ready-made' marine engine, there should be little for the installer to worry about, so he can concentrate on making a good job of fixing it into the boat. A virtually 'tailor-made' specification can be ordered from the maker's catalogue to suit the boat, and with the engine most firms will provide installation drawings, wiring diagrams and advice on operation, choice of propellers, etc. If anything goes wrong in service there is a warranty and spare parts service which, for the larger engine manufacturers, extends to most countries in the world—very useful for boats going abroad, or boat-builders in the export business.

Unless the cost of a 'ready-made' marine engine puts it completely out of reach, conversion is not recommended, because of the many advantages to having a manufacturer's engine—not the least being resale value of the boat. However, the next best thing is a good marinization kit fitted to a new or professionally reconditioned engine. A reputable kit supplier will give guidance and advice on the conversion of the engine to marine use, and will supply good, sound, accurately machined castings, correctly specified water pumps, coolers and other specialized equipment in corrosion-resisting materials. It is then only necessary to follow instructions carefully and ensure that components are properly assembled and accurately aligned.

Any brackets, pipes and other items not supplied with the kit have to be made up by (or for) the marinizer—these need to be carefully produced in suitable materials able to withstand the buffeting and vibration which can be expected—especially on sea-going craft.

Cost Cutting

The ultimate in DIY marinization is achieved by purchasing the more difficult components, such as water pump and exhaust manifold and making everything else yourself or getting an experienced friend to do the welding and machining, pipe bending and brazing, etc. You may save money, but will certainly spend hours at garages and builders' merchants chasing the elusive UNF threaded setscrews or *bronze* pipe fittings, which should be used in preference to *brass* to avoid corrosion.

The specialist heat-exchanger or water-pump manufacturer may be able to supply parts for your engine, although he is not always permitted to supply the same design that he produces for the marine engine or kit manufacturer, who may have paid for the tooling and thus acquired the exclusive rights to the model you are after.

Some engines lend themselves to marinization more readily than others. Almost all petrol and diesel engines are capable of operating in a boat, but the conversion of some is difficult and hence expensive, so study the subject before rushing out to buy a secondhand van engine advertised in the local paper. In the following notes on aspects of marine design, information is given which should be helpful in avoiding pitfalls, but you must do your homework on the types of engine available in the power range you need. One way is to spend a long day at a boat show studying engines and collecting literature.

If you can obtain a new or properly reconditioned engine of a make and type which is also produced as a marine propulsion unit you are half-way to success, but beware an engine that nobody sells in marine form! Does it have an aluminium cylinder head, necessitating fresh-water cooling? Will the oil sump have to be replaced? Is it possible to drive a sea-water pump?—and so on.

Whatever engine is chosen, make sure it is in good order before installing it. Remember most boats don't give you much room for complex engine repairs, and engine removal is usually a time-consuming job.

In Chapter 2 I referred to liquid versus air cooling. For the marinizer the small range of air-cooled engines available to him—diesel or petrol—and the difficulties of installing air ducts, etc make liquid cooling preferable, so we will assume that this choice has been made and concentrate on marinization of water-cooled engines.

I have seen boats on inland waterways where cost-cutting was taken to the limit by removing an engine and gearbox from a car and virtually dropping them straight into the boat. They should have been dropped into the water!

Inadequate cooling, fire risks, lubrication problems, corrosion, difficult reversing, poor propeller efficiency could all be anticipated, however well the engine may have been installed.

Marine Operating Requirements

The differences between a marine engine and its land-based counterpart are due largely to the working environment and operating conditions. The boat engine will probably be inclined in the fore-and-aft plane from about 10 to 15 degrees or more, so the lubrication system, the oil sump and oil pump must cater for this. The sump will be close to the bottom of the hull, so that the oil cannot be drained away. There will, therefore, be no cooling airflow over the sump, so that other means of cooling the oil must be provided.

Perhaps the most important difference is that a radiator and fan will not work inside the engine compartment. However, as the sea (or river, etc) provides a convenient supply of cooling water a special system with a pump able to handle this often gritty and corrosive fluid is employed. If air cooling is used, ducting to carry the air to and from the engine will be required.

A reversing transmission with possibly a speed-reduction gearbox will be interposed between the engine and the drive to the propeller. This can be accomplished in many different ways, as shown in Chapters 1 and 4.

Petrol engines need a carburettor which will function at sea and all types of engine must be protected against corrosion. These and other aspects of the marine engine are dealt with in more detail in the following pages.

COOLING SYSTEM

Cooling is one of the most important features of a marine engine. Liquid-cooled engines make use of the water in which the boat is floating, in the following ways.

Direct Cooling

This is the simplest arrangement with a positive displacement pump drawing in water, passing it through the engine water-jackets and oil coolers, etc, then discharging overboard (Fig 40). A recirculating arrangement with a manually or thermostatically operated control valve is sometimes used to maintain water flow through the cylinder head at a rate which enables combustion to take place at a suitable temperature. Overcooling makes for noisy, inefficient combustion in diesel or petrol

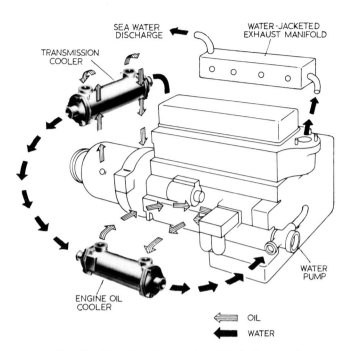

Fig 40   Direct cooling system (*E. J. Bowman*)

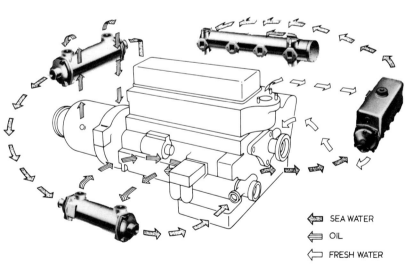

Fig 41   Heat exchanger cooling system with coolers and heat exchangers detached for clarity (*E. J. Bowman*)

77

motors, increasing fuel consumption and the formation of soot and other undesirable products of combustion. This arrangement is only suitable for operation in clean, fresh water as when sea water is used the direct-cooling system has to cope with sand in suspension, as well as the deposition of salts in the water-jackets if a temperature of about 63°C (145°F) is exceeded. Even in fresh water the system is vulnerable to blockage of the inlet pipe, which will cause overheating within a minute.

Heat-Exchanger Cooling
Two circuits are used in this system. The primary one, generally referred to as the 'raw' water circuit, utilizes a positive-displacement pump which draws in water, passes it through the heat exchanger and possibly through the lubricating oil and transmission oil coolers, and then discharges it overboard (Fig 41). Usually no attempt is made to control the flow of water around the primary circuit.

The water pump employed by the secondary circuit circulates coolant through the engine water-jackets and then passes it on to the heat exchanger, where it is cooled by the tube stack through which the cold water from the primary circuit is being pumped. A centrifugal type of pump is often used in this circuit as it is not necessary to develop much pressure to carry out the process.

This circuit is completely self-contained; it is topped up when necessary by adding fresh water to the header tank, which is used to de-aerate the water as it is churned up in passing rapidly round the circuit. Some engines employ a sealed system similar to that used in car engines. The secondary circuit is usually pressurized by means of a pressure cap on the header tank or sealed-system reservoir. This has the effect of raising the boiling point and thus allowing a smaller heat exchanger to be used.

Control of the temperature level in the secondary circuit is maintained by a thermostatic valve which is generally activated by a wax capsule. While the engine is warming up flow by-passes the heat exchanger to speed the warm-up period, the valve then opens, the bypass is closed off and the main flow passes through the heat exchanger (Fig 42). Under full-load summer conditions almost all of the water will pass through

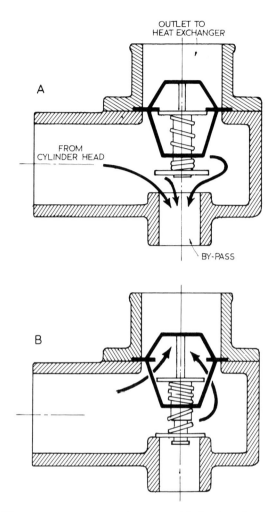

OUTLET TO
HEAT EXCHANGER

A

FROM
CYLINDER HEAD

BY-PASS

B

Fig 42 Thermostat: wax capsule type with bottom by-pass valve:
A – thermostat closed during 'warm-up' with flow through bypass;
B – thermostat open, main flow to heat exchanger and by-pass closed

the thermostat valve, but under colder or part-load conditions
the valve will allow some flow to be bypassed and thus prevent
overcooling.

Keel Cooling
This system got its name from its main feature—pipes

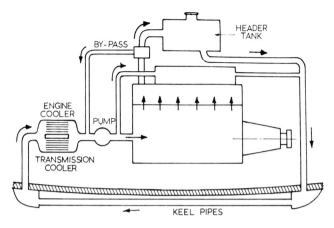

Fig 43   Keel cooling system

running close to the sides of the keel. As Fig 43 shows, it is in effect a heat-exchanger system where the primary circuit is replaced by the sea, and the heat-exchanger tube stack is replaced by the keel pipes. The main reason for using keel cooling is that it gives the engine corrosion-free fresh-water circulation with efficient thermostatic control, but without the need for bringing any sea water into the boat. It is therefore possible to operate this system in very corrosive or silty water without danger of corrosion or blockages in the raw water circuit. This means, however, that the oil coolers have to operate with fresh water, and therefore they have to be somewhat larger. As there is no water available for injection into the exhaust pipe, either a small pump has to be employed especially for this function or a dry exhaust system has to be used. Incidentally, keel-cooling systems are not easy to empty, so that antifreeze is needed even if the boat is laid up in the winter.

Skin-Tank Cooling
A variation on keel pipes that is particularly suitable for aluminium hulls is provided by forming skin tanks on the inside of the hull. Two of the disadvantages of keel pipes—vulnerability to damage and additional drag—are eliminated because there is no external evidence of skin cooling when it is arranged in this way.

80

Air Cooling

This arrangement employs a fan to direct air over the finned surfaces of the cylinder head and block, and also over the coolers (Fig 44). Efficient ducting has to be arranged to conduct air to and from the engine; adequate insulation is needed to avoid fires caused by heat radiated from the hot engine surfaces.

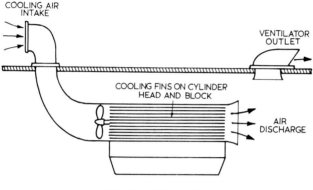

Fig 44   Air cooling

COOLING SYSTEM COMPONENTS

We will now look at some of the components used in the cooling systems described above, starting with one of the most difficult to produce satisfactorily.

Water-cooled Exhaust Manifold

The coolant may be either sea water or fresh water—possibly with antifreeze added. The material used for the water-jacket has to be compatible with the coolant used. If aluminium is used, it should be of a corrosion-resistant specification such as BS 1490 LM6M, although even this material may corrode if there are copper pipes in the circuit and sea water is used as the coolant. So unless weight is very important cast iron is a better material to use, or even bronze if the high cost of this metal is acceptable. Welded stainless-steel fabrications are also satisfactory and eliminate the cost of pattern equipment, but they tend to be expensive in comparison with an aluminium or iron casting (Fig 45).

81

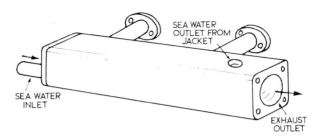

Fig 45   Exhaust manifold

Foundries specialize in particular types of casting, and several have overcome the problems of producing water-jacketed manifolds without the blocked coolant passages and uneven wall thicknesses that cause cracks in service or even before the engine runs. Of course, the design of the manifold is as important as good foundry techniques; there should be proper provision for core supports and all water spaces must be as generous as space allows.

It is not recommended that the marinizer should try to fabricate a mild-steel manifold or weld a jacket over the original engine component. Neither should he wrap the 'dry' manifold with asbestos tape in the hope that it will not set fire to the engine compartment. The petrol engine exhaust at full load can attain more than 750°C (1380°F), while the diesel exhaust will be about 100°C (180°F) lower if naturally aspirated, and lower still if turbocharged.

Sea-Water Pump

With the exception of ships' lifeboat engines, which have to run dry for a short period while the engine is started in the davits, a rubber impeller type pump is the most convenient. Most vane and gear pumps will wear out more quickly than a rubber impeller pump when used on boats operating in shallow, silty water.

Proprietary pumps are manufactured in a range of models, with the nominal size based upon the bore of the inlet and outlet connections. Imperial sizes are standard for pumps produced in the UK and the USA, $\frac{1}{2}$, $\frac{3}{4}$, 1 and $1\frac{1}{4}$in sizes being used for most engines in the 20 to 200bhp (15 to 150kW) range.

82

The action of the rubber impeller (Fig 46) generates considerable pressure, so that connecting hoses and pipes must be capable of withstanding the effects of pressure build-up in the circuit caused by accidental blockages. Similarly the suction head generated can cause the collapse of soft intake hoses.

Purpose-built engines will have provision for a shaft drive for the sea-water pump. A typical rubber impeller pump is shown in Plate 45, which depicts one of the JABSCO pump models.

Unless they are able to make use of a power take-off intended for a compressor, etc, marinized engines have to use a belt drive to power the sea-water pump—usually from the crankshaft pulley. For direct-cooled engines, where the only auxiliaries to be driven are the alternator and sea-water pump,

Flexible impeller blades, upon leaving offset cam, create a nearly perfect vacuum for instant self-priming.

As impeller rotates, each successive blade draws in liquid and carries it from intake to outlet port.

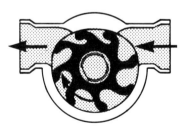

When flexible impeller blades again contact the offset cam they bend with a squeezing action that provides a continuous, uniform flow.

Fig 46   Action of impeller (See Plate 22) (*Jabsco*)

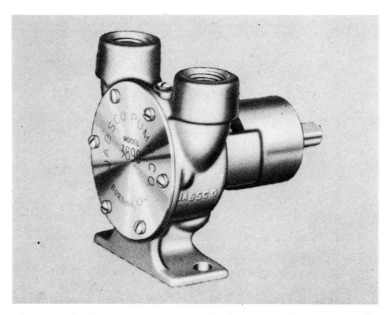

Plate 22 JABSCO sea-water pump showing removable end plate for access to rubber impeller

tension can be applied to the belt (or twin belts for larger engines) by the alternator on its adjustable bracket.

If the crankshaft pulley does not have an additional sheave for the sea-water pump drive belt, and there is no provision for attaching an additional pulley, the best plan for the do-it-yourselfer is to obtain a special pulley with the extra groove from a kit supplier or an engine dealer.

The sea-water pump speed will depend on the engine-rated speed and the belt-drive ratio. Unless there is a marinized engine available to show him the details required, the do-it-yourselfer will have to check these items with the pump supplier.

A convenient means of mounting a belt-driven sea-water pump is by attaching it to one of the engine front-mounting brackets, on which a platform is provided with slotted holes for belt adjustment.

Fresh-Water Pump
When heat-exchanger cooling is used, the original engine water

pump is generally retained for fresh-water circulation. The triangulated belt drive from crankshaft pulley to water pump and alternator is also retained. It is then necessary to have a separate belt drive to the sea-water pump (Fig 47). This applies to converted engines and most marine engines derived from automotive models.

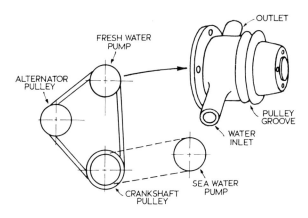

Fig 47   Fresh water pump

Heat Exchanger

This item is either tailor-made, so that its shape blends in with the lines of the engine, or is a standard off-the-shelf assembly made in a range of sizes according to engine power. In the latter case it will need support brackets and pipe fittings to connect it to the fresh– and sea–water circuits. It will include a tube 'bundle' and a header tank, either incorporated in the main casting or mounted separately. For the do-it-yourselfer the combined heat exchanger and exhaust manifold—if obtainable for the engine in question—is the best bet, because it considerably simplifies his job by minimizing the pipes, brackets and other fittings required.

Plates 23, 24 and 25 show two types of heat exchanger from E. J. Bowman, also the 'multicooler' used by Perkins on their 'Range 4' six-cylinder models where, as well as the heat exchanger, header tank and manifold being combined, the induction manifold and thermostat assembly are also included.

85

Above
Plate 23 Bowman standard type heat exchangers for engines up to 300bhp (225KW)

Below
Plate 24 Perkins 'multicooler' assembly for Range 4 engines

Opposite above
Plate 25 Bowman combined heat exchanger/exhaust manifold for Mercedes–Benz OM 636 engine

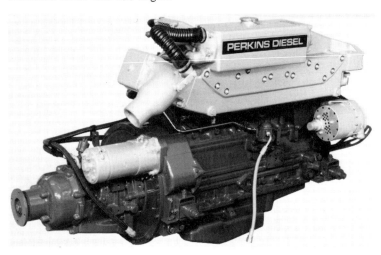

Water Pipes

Solid-drawn copper tubing is the best material, and 'Yorkshire' type copper fittings are useful for small-diameter pipes to avoid forming tight bends. Avoid brass fittings which will corrode in sea water. Moulded rubber hoses may be convenient for the larger fresh-water pipes, but they must be reinforced when used on the suction side of the water pump to prevent them collapsing. Rubber 'radiator' hose (except for short connecting lengths with hose clips) should not be used on the suction side of the sea-water pump where it will be liable to collapse. Good-quality stainless-steel hose clips should be used—preferably the worm-drive type (Fig 48).

Steel pipes are suitable for the fresh-water circuit, but they

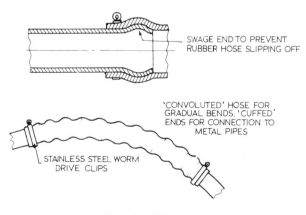

SWAGE END TO PREVENT RUBBER HOSE SLIPPING OFF

'CONVOLUTED' HOSE FOR GRADUAL BENDS, 'CUFFED' ENDS FOR CONNECTION TO METAL PIPES

STAINLESS STEEL WORM DRIVE CLIPS

Fig 48   Water   pipe

87

must be carefully painted externally to avoid sea-water corrosion.

Water Injection Bend
As well as matching the exhaust-manifold flange, this has to suit the run of the exhaust pipe. The water connection from the engine outlet may be either an internal passage through the mating flanges or an external pipe. Cast iron or a stainless-steel fabrication is generally used—sometimes with an angular adjustment at the flange provided by a swivelling joint or slotted holes when the flange is circular.

Mild-steel bends are not advisable, as they are difficult to galvanize or plate internally and will corrode rapidly.

The bore of the 'dry' part of the bend should be at least equal to the manifold bore, and the diameter should increase by half an inch or an inch where the water is injected. The outside diameter of the snout should match the bore of the diesel exhaust hose, ie 2, $2\frac{1}{2}$, 3, $3\frac{1}{2}$in, etc. Note that the water-injection section (Fig 49) should be positioned so that water cannot get into the exhaust manifold whatever angle it is installed at.

Engine manufacturers specify the maximum back-pressure that can be exerted on the exhaust system. The water-injection bend plus exhaust hose must not exceed this pressure, otherwise there will be a loss of power and, where diesel engines are used, an increase in smoke emission.

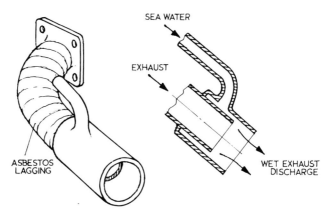

Fig 49   Water injection bend

88

Lubricating Oil Cooler

Most marine engines are designed for world-wide operation, consequently the oil cooler fitted will generally be larger than is necessary to cool the lubricating oil under temperate conditions. The do-it-yourselfer can usually manage with a smaller cooler if his area of operations is restricted to home waters, especially if the engine is not to be operated at maximum revs—a condition for which the standard production model must provide.

To simplify pipework and prevent the overloading of the engine fresh-water pump, marinizers using heat-exchanger cooling systems should fit the cooler in the sea-water circuit. Another advantage of doing this is that the size of the unit can be kept down to a minimum, because the lower temperature of sea water compared with fresh water makes the unit much more efficient. Of course direct-cooled engines give no choice of position for the cooler.

Some engines that are used intermittently at low revs and have a generous oil-sump capacity may operate satisfactorily without a cooler. This can be established during trials, but room must be provided in the engine compartment for the cooler, pipes and repositioned lubricating oil filter, if these are found to be necessary.

Flexible high-pressure pipe assemblies are recommended for the pipes from engine supply to cooler and from cooler

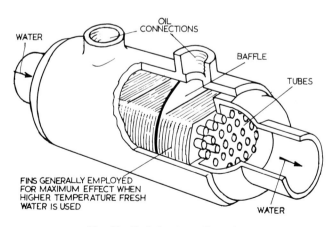

Fig 50   Lubricating oil cooler

89

to lubricating oil filter. These pipes have to be capable of withstanding about four times the maximum working oil pressure, and the high pressure experienced for a short period when starting from cold. To reduce the pressure loss through the oil pipes the diameter of the bore should not be less than that of the holes in the filter head. The bore of the pipe end fittings should be only slightly less than that of the pipe itself.

Lubricating Oil Filter

To enable the engine oil to be piped to and from the cooler it is necessary to fit an adaptor between the filter and the cylinder block with connections from the cooler pipes. Some 'marinizations' include a purpose-made cooler sandwiched behind the original oil filter. This is a better arrangement because the oil pipes are then eliminated. Plate 26 shows a Dex marine engine with built-on cooler.

Transmission Oil Cooler

The size of this item will be prescribed by the transmission manufacturer according to the power and speed of the engine. Direct-drive units, unless they are of the Layshaft design,

Plate 26 Dex marine engine. Arrow indicates built-on oil cooler which eliminates oil pipes

generally dissipate less heat than reduction-gear models, so that a smaller cooler can be used.

The remarks concerning oil pipes and connections for the engine cooler also apply to the transmission cooler.

LUBRICATION

The lubrication system of an engine installed in a boat can differ in several ways from a land-based system. A cooler is used to maintain the oil temperature below the engine manufacturer's maximum. The temperature is usually measured in the 'pressure rail' of the cylinder block where oil is ducted to the bearings.

Keeping this measurement within the maker's maximum helps to maintain satisfactory lubrication at critical points such as the main and big-end bearings and the piston-ring grooves. Prescribed temperatures are usually between 110°C and 132°C (230°F and 270°F). A typical circuit is shown in Fig 51.

When an engine operates in very cold conditions the oil may be overcooled and become too viscous for effective lubrication. A special thermostat combined with a relief valve, such as the 'Vernatherm' valve, may then be built into the lubrication system.

The oil sump should be of corrosion-resistant material or should be treated by coating it with plastic, because it may occasionally dip in the bilge water. There must be provision

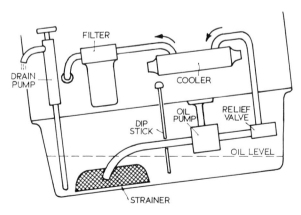

Fig 51   Lubrication system

for a drain connection so that the oil can be drawn out by a drain pump.

Although there are various coupling devices and transmissions designed to allow the engine to operate in a more-or-less horizontal plane while the propeller shaft is angled at about 10 to 15 degrees, most engines are installed inline with the shaft, so designs must cater for this requirement. This means the oil sump has to be positioned in such a way that the end of the pick-up pipe is completely immersed at any angle between zero and about 18 to 20 degrees, because most boats under way will trim down by the stern a further 3° or so. With vee-drives the engine is installed the other way round, so that when installed horizontally the engine will operate with its front end down about 3° when the craft is under way.

A further requirement, which affects the cooling system as well as the sump, exists for auxiliary yacht and motor-sailer installations in which engines are sometimes used while the craft is beating to windward heeled over at about 30°. The pipes and tanks, etc must be designed so that airlocks do not occur at extreme angles of inclination, nor when the boat is rolling or pitching violently.

The lubricating oil filter must be positioned above the engine beds, so that it is accessible in the installation. This often necessitates the use of an inverted filter or repositioning the filter higher up on a bracket with pipes (generally flexible to avoid vibration problems) connecting up with the engine and the oil cooler.

AIR FILTER

Strictly speaking, marine engines do not need air filters, because very little dust is encountered at sea. However, some boats operate on inland waterways, harbours and other areas where dust is present, and there may be dusty cargoes to contend with.

A quick look over a group of engines at a boat show would indicate that some have simple gauze screens on the air inlet, while others have paper-element air cleaners. The oil-bath air cleaner is not very common nowadays, nor is the oil-wetted type.

A modern design of paper-element air cleaner is used on the Volvo Penta MD 40 engine, and is illustrated in Plate 27.

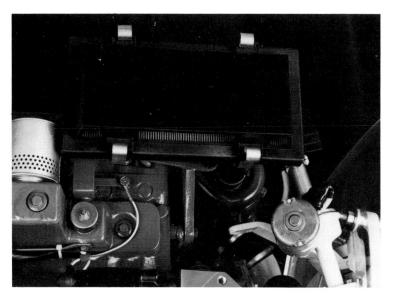

Plate 27 Air filter silencer, paper element type, shown on a Volvo Penta AQD 40/280 engine

BACKEND

This comprises the flywheel, starter-gear ring, the coupling to transmit power to the transmission and the flywheel housing, which for boat engines generally supports the transmission and carries the engine rear-support brackets.

The flywheel is bolted to the crankshaft 'palm' and carries the starter-gear ring—usually a shrink fit on its periphery. The size of the flywheel is governed by several factors. It must be of sufficient mass—usually expressed as its 'moment of inertia'—to smooth out the irregular motion of the crankshaft. The more cylinders there are in the engine, the less need there is for flywheel effect. The marinizer will usually make use of a standard flywheel, but may have to drill and tap holes in the rear face for the coupling.

The coupling cushions the drive to the transmission by means of rubber or springs incorporated in the assembly. A common type used with transmissions such as Borg Warner, Hurth, Paragon, Self-Changing Gears, Twin Disc, ZF, etc is the damper drive coupling which is illustrated in Fig 52 with a typical backend assembly. The springs which control the

93

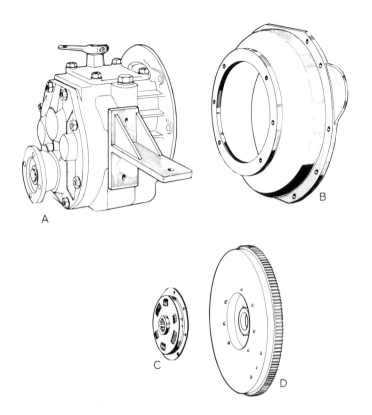

Fig 52 Back end assembly – Arona engines: A reverse-reduction gearbox with engine rear support brackets; B flywheel housing (Bell housing type); C damper drive coupling; D flywheel with starter gear ring

relative movement of the mounting flange and the splined hub are varied to suit the engine torque. Transmission manufacturers will recommend a suitable damper drive coupling for any approved engine adaption.

The flywheel housing should provide a water-tight enclosure and have side facings for the engine rear-support brackets. Two forms of housing are common:

1   Open rear end with the front end bolted to the engine block. An adaptor plate may be required for transmission attachment.

2   Bell housing type with a backplate attached to the

94

engine block and the front face machined for attachment of the transmission.

The engine side of the housing (or backplate in the case of the bell housing arrangement) is machined to take the mounting flange of the starter motor.

Alignment of the backend components is vital to prevent the transmission bearings and possibly the engine rear main bearing wearing out prematurely. The engine maker will quote the limits of eccentricity for the flywheel housing rear spigot with the crankshaft palm or a recess in the flywheel. This has to be carefully checked with a dial indicator when assembling the backend components, and it may be necessary to dowel the flywheel housing to the engine block when correctly aligned.

Stiffness of the engine and transmission assembly is affected by the design of the flywheel housing. For maximum rigidity of the engine structure and minimal vibration transmission it is good practice to bolt the flywheel housing to a flange at the rear of the sump. This is even more important for engines where the cylinder block 'skirt' does not extend below the crankshaft centreline.

ENGINE SUPPORT

Four brackets cantilevered from the sides of the engine—two

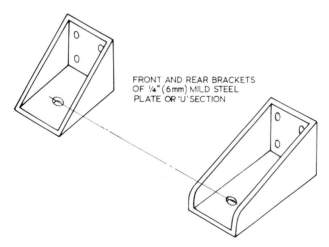

FRONT AND REAR BRACKETS OF ¼" (6 mm) MILD STEEL PLATE OR 'U' SECTION

Fig 53 Engine support brackets

at the front end of the cylinder block and two on the fly-wheel-housing side facings or the transmission casing are the usual arrangement. With very heavy built-on transmissions two additional supports at the rear end may be needed.

Chapter 4 deals with engine seating and the use of resilient engine mountings between the support brackets and the engine beds.

In designing engine support brackets one should bear in mind that forces of 6g can occur under storm conditions. Fig 53 shows a set of brackets fabricated from mild steel.

POWER TAKE-OFF

Although some marine engines have provision for power take-off drives from the timing gears or the transmission, the majority of engines applied to boats rely on a drive from the front of the crankshaft. Engines with belt-driven auxiliaries, eg, water pump and alternator, have a crankshaft pulley to which the means of transmitting the drive is attached.

The amount of power (expressed as torque) which can be used depends on the way in which the pulley is attached to the crankshaft. An automotive-type engine may have only a small key for pulley location, whereas an engine built for marine use will have a splined or tapered end or other method of attachment capable of transmitting the full engine torque.

Fig 54 shows three systems as used for fishing boats and other working craft.

1 Additional pulley bolted to the crankshaft pulley. This is the simplest arrangement for belt-driving winches, small generators, compressors, etc. The direction and magnitude of the belt pull is of importance, as there is a limit to the 'bending moment' that can be imposed on the crankshaft. Two equal belt drives diametrically opposed to each other will cancel out the bending moment; this is therefore the preferable arrangement. Another important factor which may limit this arrangement is the amount of overhanging weight from the additional pulley.

2 An axial drive to a generator, etc which is mounted forward of and in line with the crankshaft pulley. A flexible coupling is recommended for attachment to the crank pulley to allow for a slight misalignment and also to help

96

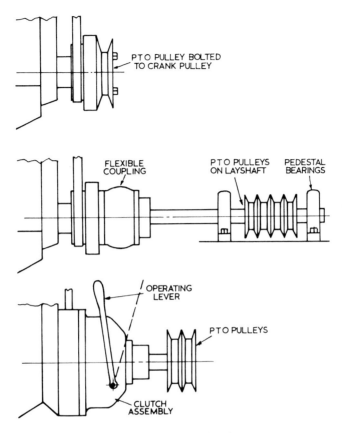

Fig 54 Power take-off drives

damp-out drive line vibrations. The Fenner 'tyre-type' coupling is suitable and is available in a range of sizes to match the power take-off.

When belt drives are outside the capacity of a bolted-on pulley, a layshaft can be provided mounted in bearings with a flexible coupling.

3 A clutch power take-off mounted on the front of the engine. This arrangement is most suitable for engines without belt-driven auxiliaries because the clutch assembly has to be removed in order to replace the belts.

A mechanical 'over-centre' type clutch is the most common type in use. Twin Disc, for example, provide a

97

range of clutches with SAE standard flanges to match the housing which is attached to the front of the engine.

Torsional Vibration

'TV' was referred to by marine-engine installers long before the small screen appeared in our living rooms. Torsional vibrations occurring in the crankshaft can cause failure of this important component or of the couplings and other parts of the power take-off assembly.

The likelihood of this vibration being excessive in service can be calculated by making a layout of the complete engine and its installation, starting with the front-end power take-off drive and couplings, pulleys, etc, the engine, flywheel, transmission, propeller shafting and couplings, then the propeller. The 'moment of inertia' and 'stiffness' of all parts of this system are then established, including the 'entrained water' which is carried round by the propeller. With the aid of a computer, the stresses in various parts of the system can be calculated, as can the 'critical speeds', ie resonant conditions, which must be passed through quickly if they occur within the engine operating-speed range.

One way of minimizing torsional vibration is to fit a TV damper, which has the effect of 'detuning' the system and reducing the amplitude of vibrations that occur. A 'viscous'

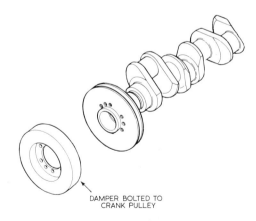

DAMPER BOLTED TO
CRANK PULLEY

Fig 55 Torsional vibration damper

98

damper is often used for this purpose on marine engines. It is usually attached to the crankshaft pulley.

Fortunately most installations with modest front-end drives will not have torsional-vibration problems, provided that excessively heavy pulleys or couplings and belt loadings are avoided. If in doubt, it is best to contact the engine supplier before committing yourself to the power take-off arrangement.

Transmissions

Except when a controllable-pitch reversing propeller or a water jet is driven by the engine, a reversing or reversing/reduction gearbox is required. Various propeller-shaft layouts are shown in Chapter 1 and numerous types of transmission are available to suit them. The most common designs of transmission are as follows.

Plate 28 Reverse-reduction gearbox. Drop-centre type with mechanically operated clutch on output shaft. Hurth model HBW 15

DROP-CENTRE REVERSE/REDUCTION GEAR

Two trains of gears in constant mesh connect the input and output shafts. The clutch engages with either train to give forward or reverse rotation, both trains are disengaged for neutral. A direct drive ratio or reduction may be incorporated in the gearing and usually, in twin-engine installations, left- and right-handed output shaft rotation is obtainable from the same engine rotation by using the two pinions for one engine and the three pinions for the other in forward gear. Various types of clutch can be provided—mechanical with friction plates, mechanical with an automotive-type synchromesh unit, electro-magnetic or hydraulic.

COAXIAL REVERSE GEAR

In this design use is made of a clutch-operated epicyclic gear train to provide the three conditions—ahead, neutral and astern. In ahead gear the running-gear assembly is locked up and rotates *en masse*; in neutral the input end rotates with the engine while the output end is stationary; in astern gear the annulus is locked to the casing and the planetary gears rotate on their axis so that the output shaft turns in the opposite direction to the input. This design is used by several manufacturers with mechanical and hydraulic clutches, and gives a 1 : 1 ratio in forward gear. There is usually a reduced speed in astern gear, due to the geometry of the epicyclic gear train which has to fit into the space available.

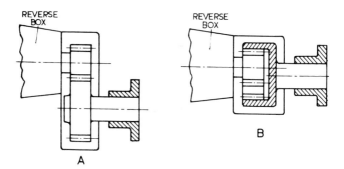

Fig 56 Reduction gears: A two- or three-pinion gear train; B two-pinion gear train using internal gear to minimize difference in input and output shaft centres

100

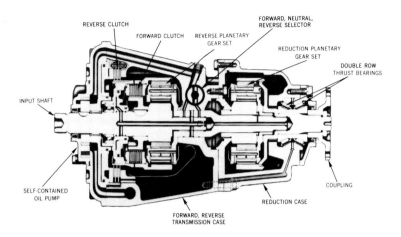

REVERSE CLUTCH
FORWARD CLUTCH
REVERSE PLANETARY GEAR SET
FORWARD, NEUTRAL, REVERSE SELECTOR
REDUCTION PLANETARY GEAR SET
DOUBLE ROW THRUST BEARINGS
INPUT SHAFT
SELF-CONTAINED OIL PUMP
COUPLING
REDUCTION CASE
FORWARD, REVERSE TRANSMISSION CASE

Plate 29 Borg Warner 'velvet drive' reverse-reduction gearbox

Plate 30 Hydraulically-operated reverse-reduction gearbox. Self-changing Gears Ltd, MRF 500 MK II. Heavy duty transmission with offset output shaft

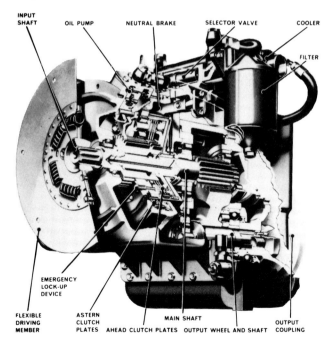

INPUT SHAFT
OIL PUMP
NEUTRAL BRAKE
SELECTOR VALVE
COOLER
FILTER

EMERGENCY LOCK-UP DEVICE

FLEXIBLE DRIVING MEMBER
ASTERN CLUTCH PLATES
AHEAD CLUTCH PLATES
MAIN SHAFT
OUTPUT WHEEL AND SHAFT
OUTPUT COUPLING

CUT-AWAY VIEW OF MRF 500 Mk II MARINE GEARBOX

101

An 'add-on' reduction gear (see Plate 29 and Fig 56) can be applied to the coaxial box in two ways giving either a coaxial output shaft by using another epicyclic train in constant mesh or a simple two- or three-pinion drive, according to the direction of output-shaft rotation required.

Engine Controls

Apart from launch engines which have a mechanical gearbox necessitating manual operation of the gear lever, most boat engines have a 'single-lever' throttle and gearchange system. As Fig 57 shows, a continuous movement will take you from full speed ahead to full speed astern with intermediate throttle positions in either direction or in neutral gear. This is accomplished by a linkage in the control head with push–pull cables to the engine throttle and gearchange lever. Alternative systems with electrical, hydraulic and pneumatic actuation are available.

For boats with twin control positions, it is possible to have dual single-lever controls. Two cables then operate the throttle and gearchange—special adaption kits allow smooth operation from either control location. For twin-engine boats it is

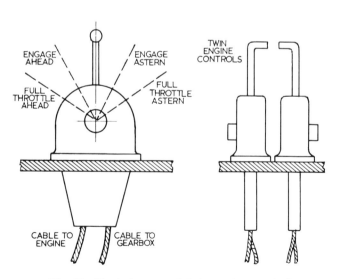

Fig 57 Single-lever and twin engine controls

possible to control both engines simultaneously with one hand when the controls are mounted side by side.

Corrosion

In selecting and manufacturing marine components, materials that will not corrode should be chosen. This applies particularly to valves, pipes and fittings in the cooling systems, but also to external parts such as the air intake where corrosion of thin steel parts could damage when sucked into the engine.

One difficulty with direct, sea-water cooling is corrosion of the cylinder-block water-jacket plugs. When these are of thin mild steel, corrosion will generally eat through in a season or so. The remedy is to remove them and replace them by stainless-steel plugs. Even when running on fresh-water cooling, occasionally topping up the system with brackish water will lead to corrosion.

Neither untreated steel, which would rust, nor brass, which is affected by dezincification, should be used in the cooling system. During dezincification, sea water removes the zinc from the alloy, leaving only the porous copper which can leak and which, if overstressed, will fracture.

Erosion can be caused by sea water flowing at a high velocity through pipes, connections, cooler end caps, etc. When this happens the protective coating that forms on many metallic surfaces is removed by the sea water (especially if silt or sand is present in suspension); the metal is then eroded and a hole eventually appears in the wall of the component.

Electrolytic corrosion caused by the use of unsuitable metals in the sea-water circuit is another hazard. (See Chapter 5).

Classification Society Approval

The approval of an engine design by societies such as Lloyds means that the 'scantlings' of the engine satisfy the design rules of the society when operating continuously at the specified power and speed. This safeguards the owner as well as the boatbuilder, preventing the use of power ratings which are too high for reliable service at sea. Principal marine-engine builders study classification society rules in advance to ensure approval of an engine before they apply for it.

4

ENGINE INSTALLATION

Preliminaries

Before getting to the stage of dangling the engine from sheer legs over the engine bearers it is advisable to do it on paper with an outline tracing of the engine to the same scale as the boat drawing. You can then check that the installation angle does not exceed the manufacturer's limit, that the engine fits into its compartment and that the service points are accessible, for example, deck beams must be clear of the oil and water filters. Having made certain that there is sufficient clearance between the engine and the bulkheads and hatch covers for soundproofing, the position and angle of the sterntube can be established, as well as the dimensions of the engine bearers. The lengths of engine controls, diesel exhaust hose, etc can be checked and ordered in good time.

Engine Seating

Timber bearers to suit the positions of the engine mountings can be made up to the shape determined by the scale drawings and 'glassed' into position. Bearers should be through-bolted to the frames and must be as rigid as possible, with cross-bracing near the engine-mounting positions. Slots to take holding-down bolts from the engine mountings should be prepared—do not use coachscrews, which can tear out of the timber in rough conditions (Fig 58).

Mountings and Couplings

Whatever the type of boat, resilient mounting of the engine

104

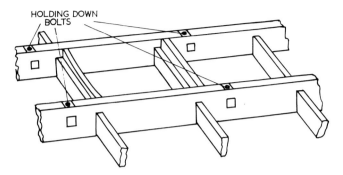

Fig 58   Timber engine seating

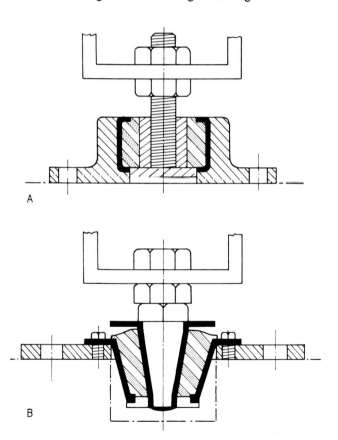

Fig 59   Resilient engine mountings: A pedestal type; B plate type
'metalastik' pattern requiring slot in engine beds for clearance

105

on flexible supports, which have been developed for the particular engine, will pay dividends in smoothness and noise reduction. It is important to use mountings with the correct hardness of rubber and deflection characteristics.

Two types of mounting are illustrated in Fig 59, both are adjustable in height to allow the engine and the propeller shaft to be accurately aligned, and to allow readjustments to be made after the rubber mountings have 'settled'. The design of these mountings allows for stresses due to accelerations of up to 6g, and also for the considerable propeller thrust which pushes the boat along via the engine mountings.

To prevent damage to the sterntube when the engine oscillates on the flexible mountings, a flexible coupling is used unless you have the particular type of sterngear described in the next section. Short, rigid shafts will require two couplings (Fig 60).

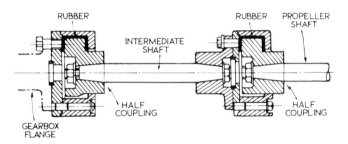

Fig 60 Twin flexible couplings Silent Bloc thrust absorbing type

Shafts and Sterngear

Shaft material is generally manganese bronze or stainless steel, sometimes monel metal. The diameter of the shaft depends mainly on the torque it has to transmit. This is the engine torque if a direct drive transmission is used. With reduction gear the torque becomes proportionately greater, ie T shaft = T engine × reduction ratio. For calculation of shaft size torque is usually expressed in bhp per 100 rev per min. For an engine producing 80 bhp at 2500 rev per min the figure is $\frac{80 \times 100}{2500}$ = 3.2 bhp per 100 rev per min. With

106

2:1 reduction gear this increases to 3.2 × 2 = 6.4 bhp per 100 rev per min.

Standard propeller shafts stocked by sterngear suppliers to the boating trade generally range from ¾in to about 2½in in the steps given in the table below.

Safe torque for manganese bronze shafts (Commercial ratings)

Diameter (in)	Bhp/100 rev/min
¾	0.3
⅞	0.8
1	1.4
1⅛	1.9
1¼	2.7
1⅜	3.7
1½	4.5
1¾	7.0
2	10.0
2¼	15.0
2½	20.0

Higher torque can be transmitted by Monel metal shafts.
(See Fig 64)

Using this table you can select an appropriate propeller shaft. If the shaft is subject to Lloyds' or other classification society rules, a larger diameter will be required. When an intermediate shaft is used a slightly smaller diameter is permissible, although in practice the need to work to the nearest stock size above your bhp figure may result in the same intermediate size as the tailshaft.

STERNGEAR ARRANGEMENTS

Many types of sterngear are available. The most popular for

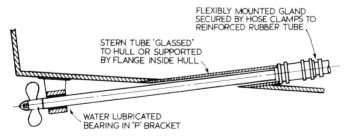

Fig 61 Typical sterngear

107

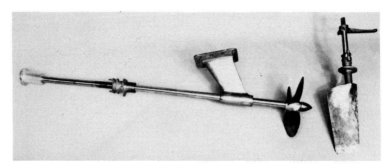

Plate 31 Propeller shaft and sterntube: typical assembly for motor launch (*Teignbridge Engineering*)

motor yachts, cruisers and runabouts, etc, consists of a shaft log and 'P' bracket (Fig 61).

With a short shaft the only bearing required is in the 'P' bracket. This is usually of rubber or polyurethane and is water lubricated. The flexibly mounted gland makes it unnecessary to have a flexible coupling in the shaft line of resiliently mounted engines.

For heavy-displacement boats and auxiliary yachts a continuous sterntube with bearings at both ends and a solidly mounted gland is usual (Fig 62). Water-lubricated bearings require a water feed from the engine sea-water pump.

Sterngear used in a wood or GRP craft is usually con-

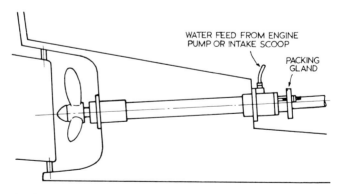

Fig 62 Sterngear installation for workboat – centreline arrangement with water-lubricated inboard bearing

structed from manganese bronze, for parts made from tube or bar, and gunmetal, for the castings. These materials are compatible with aluminium bronze or manganese bronze propellers and stainless-steel or manganese bronze shafts. It is best to check the compatibility of other material combinations with the sterngear supplier to avoid electrolytic corrosion as described in Chapter 5.

For steel hulls the propeller shaft should be of stainless steel or monel metal, the propeller should be zinc sprayed and the sterntube should be steel or cast iron zinc sprayed.

Aluminium hulls should have a stainless-steel or monel-metal propeller shaft, the propeller and sterntube should be of sea-water resisting aluminium alloy. A manganese-bronze propeller is sometimes used with zinc sacrificial anodes nearby on the hull.

Shafts and sterngear produced by established specialist suppliers can be relied upon to be accurately machined with straight true tubes and dead straight shafting. In store and transit the tubes and shafts will be carefully protected from damage, and adequately supported to prevent distortion. Shafting should never be stood on end.

PROPELLER SHAFT COUPLINGS

Whether solid or flexible, the propeller-shaft coupling is usually supplied with a pilot bore accurately centred. This has to be bored out to fit the shaft. There are several ways (Fig 63) of attaching the coupling to the shaft; the best practice is to use a taper to match the propeller end, so that if the shaft becomes worn by the stern-tube bearings it can be reversed—the worn sections should then be in a different position, away from the stern-tube bearings (unless you are extremely unlucky).

In practice, most shafts are keyed at the coupling end and secured by 'half-dog' setscrews or locking pins.

The method of preparing the shaft and coupling is:

1 Check that the shaft end is perfectly true; if not turn down by about 0.010in (0.25mm).
2 Measure shaft and bore coupling to produce a transition fit, ie approximately 0.001in (0.025mm) below shaft size.

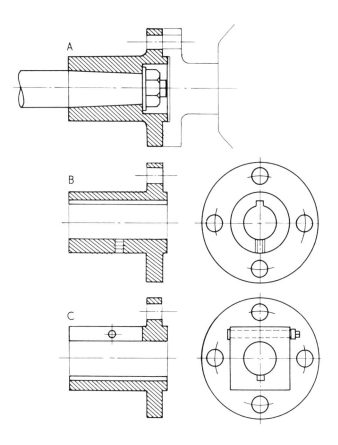

Fig 63 Propeller shaft couplings: A tapered shaft end arrangement;
B parallel bored with securing setscrew; C clamped coupling for light
duty (end-on views on right)

3 Machine a keyway in shaft and coupling to suit a flat
parallel key. Dimensions can be taken from an
engineering handbook such as Kemps' or Machinery's.
Use a $\frac{1}{4}$in square key for 1in shaft, 5/16in for 1$\frac{1}{4}$in
shaft, $\frac{3}{8}$in for 1$\frac{1}{2}$in shaft, and $\frac{1}{2}$in for 2in shaft.

4 Drill and tap two holes in the coupling as shown in
the diagram for the setscrews.

5 When the coupling is assembled on to the shaft
slightly counterbore so that the half-dog points locate
against propeller thrust.

110

Note that couplings are occasionally supplied ready bored and keywayed. When this happens, the first job is to make sure that the shaft will not be a slack fit. The best plan, if you can be sure of the length required (or can wait until the engine has been installed), is to order your shaft with coupling fitted by the sterngear manufacturer. An alternative is to use a prebored, slotted coupling as illustrated.

For a workboat application with reduction gear and high propeller-thrust loading, a tapered attachment is preferable. If the parallel system is used, a distance piece should be fitted in the coupling or the shaft end should be extended within the coupling to contact the gearbox shaft end.

SHAFT SUPPORT

In many boats the problem is how the couplings and inboard shaft gland can be fitted into the space available when the engine is positioned close to the sterntube. With the engine further forward, a longer propeller shaft may 'whirl' if the

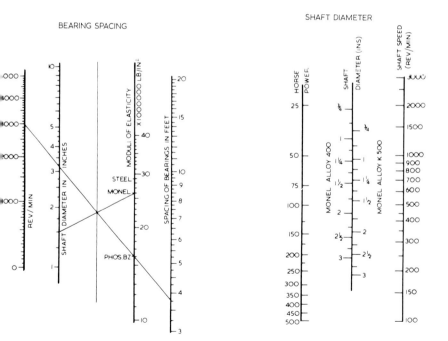

Fig 64 Bearing spacing charts

111

unsupported length between the propshaft bearings is excessive. When this occurs a plummer block should be fitted approximately mid-way along the shaft to act as a 'steady'. Very long shafts may require several support bearings.

The maximum safe unsupported length of shaft between bearings can be quickly obtained from the accompanying nomograph (Fig 64). Start by ruling a line from the shaft diameter measurement to the 'modulus of elasticity' point and note where this line cuts the blank central line. Then rule from the shaft speed on the left-hand side through the point on the central line until it cuts the right-hand scale, where you read off the safe spacing of the bearings.

Fuel Systems

Petrol or diesel engines for boats are usually supplied without a fuel tank and the interconnecting pipes, etc. It is therefore necessary to obtain satisfactory components according to the type of fuel to be used. General requirements are that the system should be liquid and vapour-tight, all parts should be properly secured and filters, cocks, etc should be accessible in the completed craft.

FUEL TANK
Almost all engines have a fuel-lift pump, so that the tank does

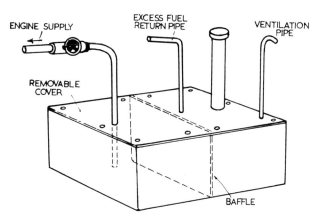

Fig 65   Fuel tank

not have to be above the engine. Materials suitable for the tanks of petrol engines are lead-coated steel, brass, copper (tin-coated internally), galvanized mild steel or monel metal. Diesel fuel tanks can be of plain steel, lead-coated steel or stainless steel. GRP of a type resistant to fuel is suitable for tanks for both petrol and diesel fuel, but check that there are no local requirements which stipulate metal fuel tanks only. There are also classification society regulations for fuel tanks, which stipulate that shut-off cocks should be secured to the tank, and that it should be possible not only to close them on the spot, but also to close them from a distance in the event of a fire in the engine compartment.

There are various design rules concerning the thickness of fueltank material, position of baffles, methods of construction, etc, but purchasing a tank from a reputable supplier of marine-engine equipment should ensure that these requirements are met.

Fuel-tank installation is also subject to various rules and regulations; for example, French law stipulates that the tank must be situated away from any sources of heat and isolated from the accommodation. Petrol tanks must be outside the engine compartment.

PIPING SYSTEM
The following points must be considered:

> elimination of possible airlocks in piping,
> prevention of dirt and water reaching the engine,
> requirements of classification societies or local authority where boat is used,
> recommendations of engine builder,
> keeping pipes away from floorboards, etc to prevent kinking,
> provision of level balancing pipe where more than one tank is used,
> secure clipping of rigid pipe and use of suitable flexible section at engine end. (Note that Lloyds approve certain types only, also that the Thames Conservancy stipulate that flexible pipe can only be used in the engine compartment.)

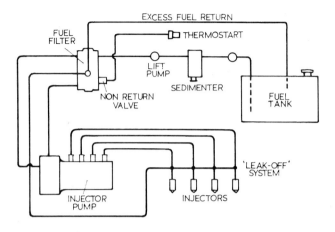

Fig 66   Typical diesel fuel system

pipe material can be softened seamless copper or copper-nickel, stainless steel or 'Bundy' for petrol or diesel.

FUEL FILTRATION

Gauze strainers are generally provided on petrol engines in the circuit between the fuel-lift pump and the carburettor. Diesel engines usually have a 'water trap' filter fitted near the tank, as shown in the circuit diagram above.

The 'sedimenter' shown in Fig 67 is an effective unit for filtering water. This may be drained off periodically from the bottom of the bowl.

Exhaust Systems

Two arrangements are used.

'Dry' exhaust—similar to that of a land-based engine, where the exhaust pipe is fitted with a silencer. The pipe generally rises vertically as shown in Fig 68.

'Wet' exhaust—sea water is discharged into the exhaust system, cooling and silencing the gas flow. In many installations, including turbocharged engines, an additional silencer is not needed (Fig 69).

114

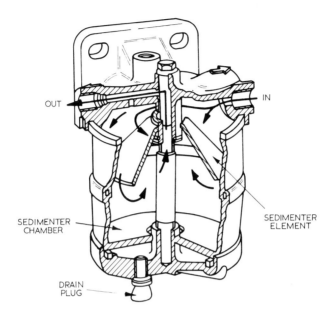

OUT

IN

SEDIMENTER CHAMBER

SEDIMENTER ELEMENT

DRAIN PLUG

Fig 67   CAV fuel sedimenter

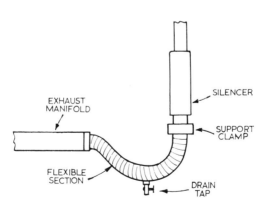

SILENCER

EXHAUST MANIFOLD

SUPPORT CLAMP

FLEXIBLE SECTION

DRAIN TAP

Fig 68   Dry exhaust system

115

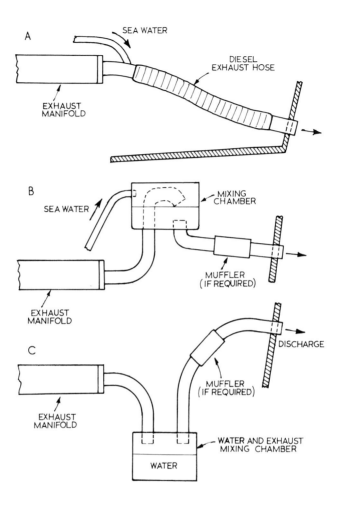

Fig 69 Exhaust systems: A standard arrangement for motor cruisers;
B high level exhaust discharge arrangement for sailcraft; C waterlock
system for installation with restricted height

BACK-PRESSURE

With all types of exhaust system the size of the fittings and
piping must be arranged so that the back-pressure on the
engine when the engine is running at full load–speed does not
exceed the maker's maximum allowable level. This figure
should be checked during trials, but as last-minute changes to

116

the exhaust system are obviously to be avoided, the size of the components must be checked out with the engine or exhaust-system suppliers before purchase.

Ventilation

Like all other aspects of engine installation, ventilation should not be an afterthought. The flow of air into and from the engine space is designed to keep the temperature at an acceptable level, to disperse fumes and, if the engine air intake is within the compartment, to provide a supply of cool, water-free air for engine breathing.

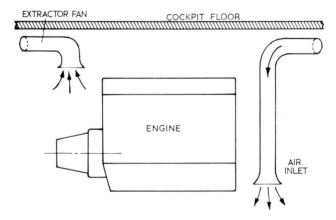

Fig 70   Ventilation of engine compartment

Forward motion of the boat will (if the position of the louvres is satisfactory) force air into the intake ducts, which should extend down to the level of the engine beds. Extractor fans are generally necessary for the outlet ducts and should pick up the air close to the top of the compartment, where it is hottest. Engine manufacturers prescribe the volume of air required by the engine per minute. This depends on the engine rated speed and its displacement. The size of the compartment is another consideration, and the table below shows the relationship of duct area to compartment volume.

117

Minimum Duct Requirements

Net compartment volume		Minimum duct diameters	
		1 intake & 1 exhaust	2 intakes & 2 exhausts
ft³	m³		
8	0.23	2in (50mm)	
12	0.34	2.5in (64mm)	
17	0.48	3in (76mm)	2.5in (64mm)
23	0.65	3.5in (89mm)	2.5in (64mm)
30	0.84	4in (102mm)	3in (76mm)
80	2.27		3in (76mm)
110	3.12		3.5in (89mm)
140	3.96		4in (102mm)
220	6.23		5in (127mm)

(Information by courtesy of Marine Engine Manufacturers' Association)

When the fuel tank is installed in a separate compartment, natural ventilation to and from the compartment should be provided. The same applies to a separate battery compartment.

Noise Reduction

Attention paid to the principles of engine-noise reduction will make the boat a much more pleasant place for the crew, as well as obviating a nuisance for others within earshot.

The general principles are to enclose the engine in a soundproof compartment by blocking up all the holes to prevent noise escaping (but in such a way that correct ventilation is not jeopardized), to prevent engine vibration being transmitted to the hull, and to minimise exhaust and induction-system noise. These principles are illustrated in Fig 71.

The inside surfaces of the compartment should have panels of sound-attenuating material attached. Proprietary 'sandwich' material of 2in (50mm) minimum thickness is recommended.

The wheelhouse and cabin floor should be covered with an absorbent material, and the roof should be lined with a proprietary noise-deadening material.

Resilient engine mountings and flexible coupling (or shaft log) will, if correctly matched to the engine, prevent excessive engine vibration being transmitted to the hull, which will amplify the sound produced.

The water-injection exhaust system should be quiet, but if

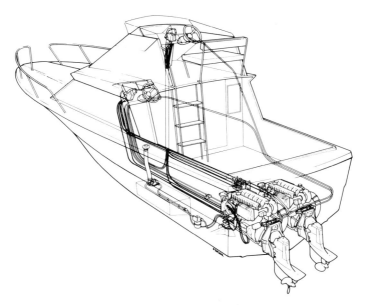

Fig 71 Noise attenuation features in twin Volvo Penta AQ D40 engines installed in soundproof compartment: flexible engine mounting, sealed pipe and cable entries, adequate ventilation, accessibility for servicing. Fuel tank is outside compartment

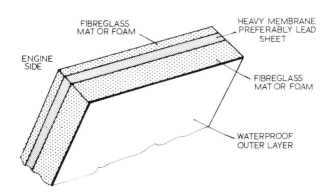

Fig 72 Sound-proofing material

119

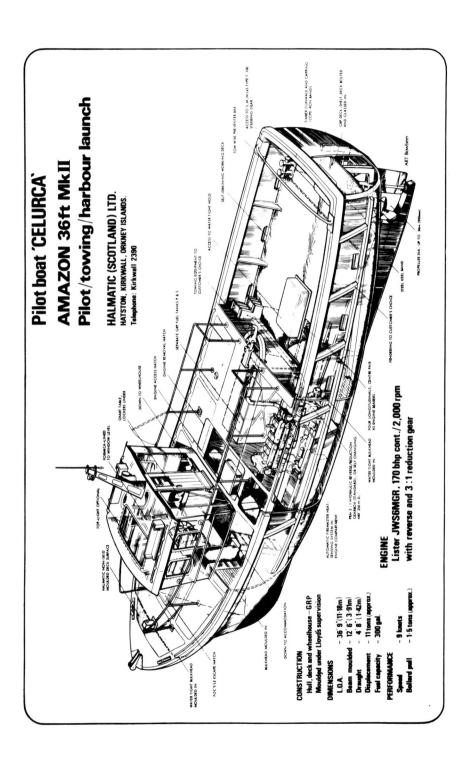

Pilot boat 'CELURCA'
AMAZON 36ft MkII
Pilot/towing/harbour launch

HALMATIC (SCOTLAND) LTD.
HATSTON, KIRKWALL, ORKNEY ISLANDS.
Telephone: Kirkwall 2390

ACCESS TO S.M. WILLS TYPE T 100
STEERING GEAR

TIMBER GUNWALE AND CAPPING
GRP. NON-BANDS

GRP DECK-SHELF. DECK BOLTED
AND GLASSED-IN

TOW WIRE PREVENTER BAR

SELF-DRAINING WORKING DECK

ACCESS TO WATER TIGHT HOLD

TOWING EQUIPMENT TO
CUSTOMER'S CHOICE

SEPARATE GRP FUEL TANKS P.& S.

ENGINE REMOVAL HATCH

ENGINE ACCESS HATCH

DOWN TO WHEELHOUSE

CHART TABLE,
LOCKERS UNDER

FORMICA-LINED
TO WINDOW LEVEL

TOP-LIGHT OPTIONAL

HALMATIC NON-SKID
MOULDED DECK SURFACE

DOWN TO ACCOMMODATION

BULKHEAD MOULDED IN

WATER TIGHT BULKHEAD
MOULDED IN

FOC'S'LE ESCAPE HATCH

AUTOMATIC FIREWATER HEAT-
SENSING SYSTEM IN
ENGINE COMPARTMENT

PKN 3. 1 HYDRAULIC REVERSE/REDUCTION
GEARBOX (STANDARD), OR SELF CHANGING
MRF 350 H.D.

WATER TIGHT BULKHEAD
MOULDED IN

FOUR LONGITUDINALS, CENTRE PAIR
AT ENGINE BEARERS.

FENDERING TO CUSTOMER'S CHOICE

STEEL KEEL BAND

PROPELLER DIA. UP TO 36in (900mm)

ART Bowbeer

ENGINE
Lister JWS6MGR, 170 bhp cont./2,000 rpm
with reverse and 3:1 reduction gear

CONSTRUCTION
Hull, deck and wheelhouse — GRP
Moulded under Lloyd's supervision

DIMENSIONS
L.O.A.	- 36'9'(11.18m)
Beam moulded	- 12'6'(3.91m)
Draught	- 4'8'(1.42m)
Displacement	- 11 tons (approx.)
Fuel capacity	- 300 gal.

PERFORMANCE
Speed	- 9 knots
Bollard pull	- 1.5 tons (approx.)

improvement is needed, a rubber muffler can be introduced in the tail pipe. Leave room for this and check it out during trials.

Some engines have an induction silencer, others need one, and a few perform satisfactorily without one—especially when the engine intake is within the compartment. Again this can be checked on trials and a silencer, which may be an ordinary paper element air cleaner with a connecting pipe to the intake, can be fitted if necessary.

Classification Societies

The principal societies which are concerned with 'machinery' installations in boats are:

American Bureau of Shipping
Bureau Veritas
Canadian Board of Steamship Inspection
Det Norske Veritas
Germanischer Lloyd
Lloyds Bureau of Shipping
Registro Italiano Navale.

There are, in addition, many government agencies and specialist organizations who act in a similar capacity, although not generally involved with pleasure craft, for example, in Britain, the Department of Trade and Industry and the White Fish Authority.

Classification societies are mainly concerned with commercial vessels. The function of those societies that are interested in the larger pleasure craft is to ensure that the engines used are designed satisfactorily for marine propulsion or 'on-board' generating sets, and that the installation is carried out in an acceptable manner with ancillary equipment, such as propeller shaft, for example, in accordance with the rules of the society.

There are various levels of classification. The highest level demands that all aspects of the design of the engine meet the

Facing page Fig 73 Workboat installation: Lister JWS GM engine in pilot/towing launch, *Celurca*

Plate 32 Twin engine installation: Ford/Sabre 365bhp engines in powerboat HTS

society's standards. The engine manufacturer has to submit drawings of the main components and technical data on cylinder pressure and bearing areas, etc to the society. If the design is acceptable, engine dynamometer tests are witnessed and, if these are OK, the engine receives design approval. Each engine produced is inspected by one of the society's surveyors at the works, and a surveyor will also check the installation in the boat.

122

5
ELECTRICS

Cables and Wiring

It is best to entrust the selection of cables, and in fact the complete wiring system of the boat, to an electrician who is experienced in marine work. The following points should be considered when planning the electrical layout.

The insulated return (two-wire) system is preferred to the single wire (earth return) used in automotive practice because a failure in the insulation of the single-wire system is more likely to cause short circuits and leakage currents which will result in electrolytic corrosion and radio interference.

Cables should be adequate for the load to be carried; stranded copper with PVC insulation of mains voltage grade is recommended. When the boat is subject to classification society rules the cable sizes specified by the appropriate society should be used.

The run of cables should be as high as possible, preferably enclosed in conduit. If not enclosed they should be secured at intervals and not allowed to drape across the engine or run along the top of engine bearers, where they can be damaged. Sources of heat such as turbochargers should be avoided. The screening of some cables will be necessary to prevent radio interference.

The engine wiring circuit will be shown on the manufacturer's wiring diagram, which also indicates auxiliary circuits for navigation and cabin lights, etc. Large craft that need electrical power for domestic appliances and boat machinery will require a separate generating set. The wiring for this will be independent of the propulsion-engine circuits.

The following table gives the maximum permissible current rating for single and two-core cables to suit Lloyds' requirements.

Nominal cross-section			Rubber or PVC		Butyl		Mineral		Resistance for 1 foot of conductor
Cable Size	sq in	sq mm	1 core	2 core	1 core	2 core	1 core	2 core	ohms
1/.044	.0015		9	7	15	12	19	16	0.00547
		1	9	7	15	12	20	17	
3/.029	.002		11	9	19	16	23	19	0.00428
		1.5	12	10	21	17	25	21	
3/.036	.003		14	11	23	19	27	23	0.00275
		2.5	17	14	27	22	31	26	
7/.029	.0045		18	16	29	24	34	29	0.00183
		4	23	19	35	29	41	35	
7/.036	.007		25	21	38	32	44	37	0.00118
		6	30	25	45	38	53	45	
7/.044	.01		31	26	48	40	56	47	0.00079
7/.052	.0145		37	31	60	51	70	59	0.00056
		10	41	34	63	53	73	62	
7/.064	.0225		51	43	78	66	93	79	0.00037
		16	54	45	83	70	99	84	
19/.044	.03		60	51	93	79	110	93	0.00029
		25	70	59	110	93	130	110	
19/.052	.04		72	61	115	96	135	115	0.00021
		35	86	73	135	115	165	140	
19/.064	.06		92	78	145	120	175	150	0.00014
		50	105	91	170	145	205	175	

(Reproduced by permission of Lucas Marine Ltd)

A typical engine wiring diagram as used for the Sabre six-cylinder engine is shown (Fig 74).

Starter Motor

Most boat engines above 30 bhp—particularly diesel ones—cannot be handstarted, and unless one of the nonelectric systems referred to in Chapter 2 is used, the electric starter has to be relied upon at all times. A marine-type waterproofed machine is preferable to an open automotive type. In order to reduce current loss in heating up starter cables that are too

124

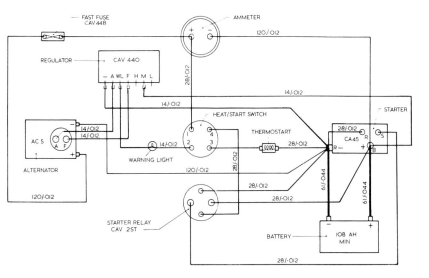

Fig 74 Engine wiring diagram, Ford/Sabre 6 cylinder

small in cross-section, the cables should always be equal to or greater than the size given in the engine wiring diagram. This is one of the most common electrical faults found in engine installations.

A solenoid is used to operate the starter. This is either mounted on the casing of the starter, built into the starter or mounted away from the starter between it and the battery.

Alternator

Although some of the more sophisticated alternators have protection against reversed polarity, most do not, so you must take care when testing the circuits and replacing the battery. Avoid short circuits across the starter terminals or regulator; do not disconnect the battery with the engine running; and de-energize the field circuit before operating the battery isolation switch.

The alternating current is converted to direct current by the built-in rectifier; the output is controlled by a regulator which is either built in or attached to the outside of the alternator

125

Plate 33 Alternators, CAV marine type machines:
(*above*) AC5, 12 volt, 60 amp; 24 volt, 30 amp;
(*below*) AC7, 24 volt, 60 amp

in the latest models. Machines of an older design have remote regulators requiring additional wiring.

Before specifying the appropriate alternator it is necessary to estimate the electrical-supply requirements. You can then decide on the size of machine required, and whether a separate one driven from the power take-off shaft or extra crankshaft-pulley groove is needed. To avoid running auxiliary yacht engines just to charge the battery, an alternator can be driven from the propeller shaft. Of course, this precludes using a folding propeller.

The maximum electrical load when under way usually occurs at night when lights are required in addition to navigation and domestic requirements.

The following is a typical peak demand for small cruisers:

lighting	12amp
radar / radio	15amp
refrigerator	7amp
pumps, fans, etc	4amp
Total	38amp

Batteries

Whether lead–acid or the more expensive alkaline types (nickel–iron) are used, the marine battery must meet two differing requirements when it supplies current to lights and other auxiliary electrical items as well as to the engine starter. A good ampere-hour rating is needed for the former, and a high discharge capability for the latter. Diesel engines may require 1000 amperes for short periods. If a separate charging plant is not used, larger boats with significant auxiliary electrical requirements should have separate batteries with a change-over switch (which should not be operated with the engine running). The engine builder specifies the size of battery required for engine starting, but the auxiliary battery depends upon the average total 'lamp load', the type of alternator and its operating speeds.

The installation of the battery is important. A separate compartment vented to allow the escape of explosive gases from a lead–acid battery is recommended. The battery should be firmly anchored to prevent movement in bad weather. Switches and fuses, etc which might produce sparks must not be located in the battery compartment. The starting battery must be close enough to the starter motor to avoid excessive voltage drop through long leads.

The temperature of the battery compartment should not exceed 50°C (122°F).

Auxiliary Equipment

Apart from equipment used in navigating the boat or looking after the creature comforts of the skipper and crew, auxiliary electrical equipment associated with the engine installation may consist of switches, fuses and relays, instrumentation, (diesel) engine starting aids, bilge pump, fuel-transfer pump, ventilation (exhaust) fans for engine and possibly the battery compartment and, of course, the ignition equipment of a petrol engine. Electrical control systems for throttle and gear change, also electric clutches within the transmission, are available, so that the modern boat can be a veritable electrical powerhouse. The ability to diagnose and correct electrical faults is often as useful to the mariner as skill in navigation.

The auxiliary equipment should be resistant to salt spray or, if in an enclosed compartment, should be resistant to the salt-laden atmosphere which attacks exposed metals when the engine is not being used. It should be able to function in the same conditions as the engine-mounted electrical equipment.

So don't be tempted to use unsuitable automotive-type equipment. Unexpected things can happen: there was once a spate of engines being started up when unattended, as though by a ghostly hand. One owner kept watch and verified that this happened on a mooring exposed to flying spray. It was found that corrosion in the switch caused a short-circuit which operated the starter relay. The ghost hunters were called off, and switches with a rubber seal in the key slot were substituted for the corroded ones.

Electrolytic Corrosion

When two dissimilar metals are immersed in an electrolyte such as sea water and connected together electrically by a conductor outside the electrolyte, a current will flow and deterioration of one of the metals will occur.

The metal on which corrosion is evident is called the 'anode'; this loses ions in the electrolyte and an electric current flows from the anode to the cathode which may be the hull or an underwater fitting of different material specification.

This phenomenon is called galvanic or electrochemical action and occurs commonly on boat fittings where different metals are used for sterngear, keel, rudder, etc. It is shown diagrammatically in Fig 75. Parts of the engine in the sea-water circuit are subject to the same corroding process, so metals used for these parts should have similar characteristics to avoid problems.

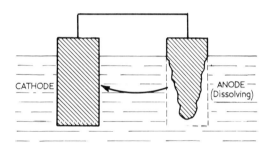

Fig 75 Electrolytic corrosion: diagramatic illustration of electro-chemical reaction showing how corrosion affects metals immersed in sea-water

The degree of corrosion occurring in the two metals depends upon the difference in voltage potential. Any metal immersed in sea water has such a potential, and where this is high it is referred to as a 'noble' metal, like gold, silver and nickel, as it will not easily corrode. It is also classified as cathodic. Conversely, the corrodible metals like magnesium, zinc and aluminium have low potential and are anodic.

The table overleaf gives the voltage potential of metals measured to the same standard conditions. When these metals are used in sea water and have a potential voltage difference of more than 0.25, corrosion can be expected.

129

Metal	Voltage potential	Metal	Voltage potential
Magnesium	−1.60	Aluminium bronze	−0.26
Zinc	−1.10	Copper	−0.25
Galvanized iron	−1.05	Monel metal	−0.20
Cadmium plating	−0.80	Nickel	−0.20
Aluminium	−0.75	Stainless steel	−0.05/−0.20
Mild steel	−0.70	Silicon bronze	−0.18
Cast iron	−0.70	Silver	0.0
Manganese bronze	−0.27	Gold	+0.15

Alloys, such as stainless steel, with varying analysis can have varying voltage potential.

Electrolytic corrosion can be caused by the leakage of electricity. Poor insulation of cables or faulty components can cause leakage to the hull with resulting corrosion. This principle can be used to prevent corrosion. If a supply of direct current is connected to the hull to make formerly anodic areas cathodic, no corrosion will occur. This system is used on large ships, but is hardly practicable for pleasure craft where sacrificial anodes are more common.

Sacrificial anodes are slabs of zinc bolted close to areas needing protection. Unless magnesium is present zinc will be eroded before any of the other metals listed in the table above. Thus the presence of zinc will protect any other materials nearby. Zinc anodes are sometimes used as plugs in the sea-water circuit of the engine to prevent corrosion of heat exchangers, manifolds, etc.

Despite taking all apparently necessary precautions, electrolytic corrosion may still appear. In this event a specialist firm can be consulted to track down the cause of the problem.

To minimize the effects of stray electric currents it is a good idea to isolate the battery when the engine is not in use.

Radio Interference Suppression

This should be planned for when laying out the wiring circuits if the radio transmitter or receiver is to be used while the engine is running. Interference can be caused by the alternator, starter motor, regulator and other engine equipment, and the electric motors, thermostats, relays, switches and light fittings,

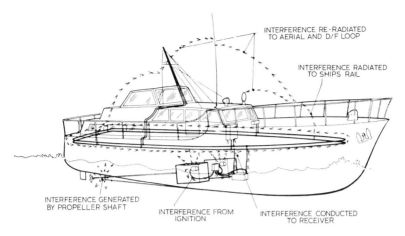

INTERFERENCE RE-RADIATED TO AERIAL AND D/F LOOP

INTERFERENCE RADIATED TO SHIPS RAIL

INTERFERENCE GENERATED BY PROPELLER SHAFT

INTERFERENCE FROM IGNITION

INTERFERENCE CONDUCTED TO RECEIVER

Fig 76   Radio interference (*Lucas Marine*)

etc in the domestic electrical systems. Even the propeller shaft and connections between the rigging and mast can cause interference, and are often difficult to find when 'trouble-shooting'. These unwanted radio signals can be eliminated or at least minimized by putting a screening enclosure around various components, using filters and bonding to a common earth.

The use of screened leads between the regulator and the control box will necessitate the use of an alternator suitably adapted to the screened conduit. A spring-loaded earthing brush can be fitted to the propeller shaft and connected to the earth circuit. Take care to avoid earthing the underwater fittings, as this may cause electrolytic corrosion.

Obviously prior experience in this field can be used to advantage in the satisfactory siting and installation of the radio equipment, as well as in the suppression of noise from the many potential sources.

Instruments

Electrically-operated instruments have largely replaced the mechanical type, due to their ease of installation at virtually any distance from the engine, and also because there is less danger of failure, as there are no interconnecting tubes to be damaged or fractured by vibration.

The following instruments are recommended to monitor the functioning of petrol or diesel engines:

engine speed tachometer,
lubricating oil pressure gauge or warning light,
water temperature gauge or warning light,
voltmeter, alternatively ammeter or charging light,
boost pressure gauge (turbocharged engines), and
transmission oil pressure gauge (hydraulic transmissions).

Dual-station instruments for use by sports fishermen, etc, with two control console positions, may be arranged by wiring in an additional panel assembly. Some makes of instruments require special sender units to operate twin sets, and sometimes require special instruments, so check with the manufacturer.

Engine Protection Equipment

Most engine manufacturers recommend the use of warning lights and audible alarms to draw attention to low oil pres-

Plate 34 Diesel engine stopping solenoid 'Synchrostart' and linkage fitted to Watermota engine (*Synchrostart*)

ELECTRICAL SYSTEM

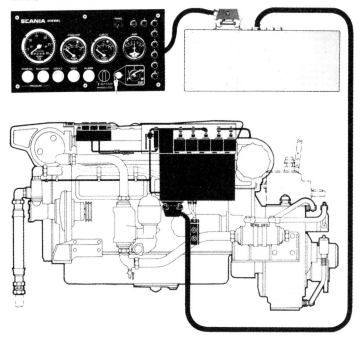

Fig 77 Engine protection equipment (*Saab-Scania*)

sure or high water temperature. The standard warning lights can be replaced by more powerful ones with a small buzzer behind the panel. A more sophisticated system is obtainable with sender units which operate on a sudden drop in oil pressure at any engine speed; similarly a sudden rise in water temperature occurring with water loss from the cooling system will actuate the high-water temperature circuit.

On-board generating-set engines that run unattended are often fitted with automatic shutdown equipment that operates on high water temperature or low oil pressure. A solenoid closes the throttle, sounds the buzzer and indicates which circuit was energized by means of the warning light.

Automatic shutdown is not acceptable on propulsion engines unless this function can be switched in or out as required, because the engine could be stopped when the boat is in a dangerous situation. The classification societies have differing rules concerning the use of automatic-shutdown equipment, so it is advisable to check the situation before planning controls and instrumentation.

Scania Marine Engines offer several variations of instrumentation, with the option of automatic-shutdown equipment. The Scania system (Fig 77) includes audible–visual alarms for coolant temperature, also engine lubricating oil, transmission hydraulic oil and sea-water pressures. There is a knob for selecting manual control or automatic shutdown when a fault has been indicated by the flashing lights and buzzer.

Most diesel engine fuel-injection systems are equipped with a stopping lever which requires a manual control for remote operation from the control position. For electrical stopping either a solenoid-operated valve is required to shut off the fuel supply or a solenoid control is connected to the fuel-pump stop lever. The latter is preferable for fast response, and is approved by most fuel-injection equipment and engine manufacturers. A 'Synchrostart' solenoid is illustrated with a typical engine adaptation in Plate 34.

6
PROPELLERS

You can spend time, energy and money on the engine for your boat, make a first-class job of the installation and then throw it all away with a badly-matched propeller. Don't be tempted, therefore, by one that 'looks about right'. You might be lucky, but are more likely to be disappointed, especially if you are choosing a propeller for a fast-planing boat.

Selection of the propeller should be made at the time you are deciding on the position of the engine and the transmission system. High-speed boats, which have a fast-turning propeller shaft will require a small propeller, and conversely a slower boat will need a relatively large, slow-turning propeller. These factors will dictate the shaft angle for the conventional installation.

Remember to allow about 15 per cent of the propeller diameter as hull clearance to avoid noise caused by the blades passing too close to the hull.

The optimum propeller for a boat is dependent on the following factors:

> engine shaft horsepower,
> propeller shaft speed,
> boat speed,
> wake factor,
> propeller aperture or space available,
> hull form,
> type of sterngear, and
> usage of boat.

The first five items on the above list affect the dimensions

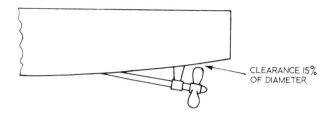

Fig 78　Propeller clearance

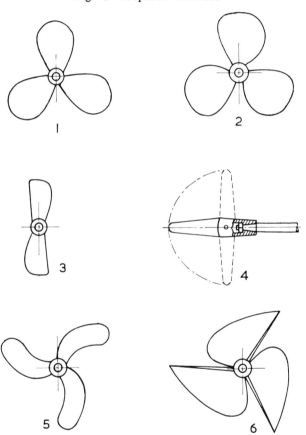

Fig 79　Typical standard propellers: 1 Turbine: general-purpose workboat and displacement pleasure craft; 2 Equipoise: high-performance design for planing boats; 3 Sailing: two-bladed propeller to be locked in vertical position; 4 Folding: for minimum resistance in racing sailboats; 5 Weedless: for inland waterways; 6 Super cavitating: for very high performance racing boats

136

of the propeller, so you can see that it is not possible to have a standard size propeller dependent merely on engine power and reduction gear ratio.

Three variables are quoted for propellers:

> diameter—simply the circle described by the tips of the blades,
>
> pitch—like a screw thread this is the theoretical distance the propeller would move forward each revolution if it was turning in a solid, and
>
> blade surface area—this can be measured by making a template of squared paper from one of the blades, counting up the number of squares to give the area, and multiplying by the number of blades.

Propeller manufacturers' catalogues list various types of propeller to suit differing types of craft and duties. Thick-bladed commercial types resistant to damage are available for heavy-duty operation, but propellers with thinner blades having sharp sections are preferable for most pleasure craft, especially high-speed planing hulls. Weedless propellers are available, also two-bladed sailing propellers, which can be feathered in the vertical plane to reduce drag. Sailing propellers which automatically fold back when not motoring are also available.

Measuring Pitch

When checking a propeller it is easy to measure diameter and even the blade surface area, but the pitch is a little more difficult to measure. The method is as follows:

> Place the propeller on a flat surface and scribe a radial line on the front face of one of the blades at about two-thirds of the radius to the tip (Fig 80). Measure off dimensions x and y, ie the heights of the points where your scribed line cuts the edges of the blade. Also measure the angle ϕ between the two points on the blade and the centre of the propeller. You can project these points onto a sheet of paper laid underneath the propeller. The pitch is then $(x—y) \times \dfrac{360}{\phi}$

137

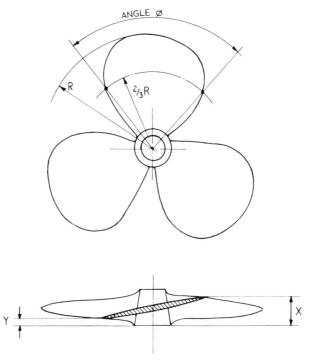

Fig 80　Propeller pitch measurement

Slip

This is the difference between the forward speed of the propeller, as though it were operating in a solid, and the speed of the boat. To be precise, this is the definition of 'apparent' slip. Because some water is dragged along by the boat (especially displacement types) 'real' slip is the difference between the forward speed of the propeller through a solid and the speed of the water ahead of the propeller. Slip percentage varies from less than 10 per cent for very fast craft to over 40 per cent for very slow boats.

Although you need to calculate slip if you are going to estimate thrust, or are concerned about the possibility of cavitation, it is not necessary to know the slip value, and indeed there is no point in trying to arrange things so that slip is reduced—it will not necessarily improve either propeller efficiency or boat performance.

138

However, this is the formula:

$$\text{slip} = \frac{(\text{pitch in feet} \times \text{shaft rev per min}) - (101.3 \times \text{speed in knots})}{\text{Pitch in feet} \times \text{shaft rev per min}}$$

How do we set about selecting the combination of number of blades, diameter, pitch and blade surface area to load the engine correctly and secure optimum boat performance? The easy way is to go to a propeller manufacturer with your boat and engine particulars and get him to work it all out for you. Alternatively, you may have access to a stock of new or good used propellers, in which case you have to arrive at a suitable specification in order to check the suitability of the sizes available.

Before getting down to the actual calculation, to demonstrate the effect of boat speed on propeller design, we will look at a series of propellers which have been calculated for the same engine power and shaft speed installed in different boats where the maximum speed at full throttle ranges from 14 to 20 knots. Although the engine power and shaft speed are the same for each boat, the optimum propeller varies with the boat speed, the diameter progressively reducing and the pitch increasing as the boat speed increases.

Boat	Boat speed (knots)	Optimum propeller dia $\times$ pitch (in inches to the nearest $\frac{1}{2}$in)
A	14	19 $\times$ 13$\frac{1}{2}$
B	15	19 $\times$ 14
C	16	19 $\times$ 14$\frac{1}{2}$
D	17	18$\frac{1}{2}$ $\times$ 15
E	18	18 $\times$ 16
F	19	18 $\times$ 16$\frac{1}{2}$
G	20	18 $\times$ 17

In each case the propeller is designed to make the best use of the engine power to achieve the fastest possible boat speed. Now what happens if we use the propeller from boat G for boat A? We certainly will not improve the speed of A. In fact, because this propeller is matched for optimum performance at a higher boat speed, the engine will be overloaded:

the revs will not reach the designed level; the power developed will be reduced and the boat speed is likely to be below 14 knots.

Conversely, if the propeller for A is used on G the engine will not be fully loaded, so it will not give full power and the boat will not attain 20 knots.

Although propellers can be made to any size, stock sizes are based on whole inch units and, except for racing craft, performance is not unduly impaired by using the nearest stock size instead of the exact measurements calculated.

Propeller Horsepower

We start by checking the shaft horsepower at the propeller. If the engine power is quoted as shaft horsepower at the gearbox output coupling, allowance has only to be made for frictional losses in propeller shaft bearings and the gland or stuffing box on the sterntube at the rate of about 1 per cent for each item. The effect of universal joints or flexible couplings is quite small and is usually ignored.

If the power was given as brake horsepower at the flywheel, a deduction must be made for the transmission losses. These will vary according to engine speed, gearbox type and whether a separate reduction gear is used. It is best to get a figure from the supplier, as the loss will range from about 2 to 15 per cent.

There is another factor which we need not worry too much about—the engine derating effect caused by high air-inlet temperature on a hot summer's day. I suggest you just accept the consequences of this phenomenon, but if you do experience a fall-off in revs with an unacceptable reduction in boat speed you can try a propeller with reduced pitch as described in chapter 7.

One further point concerning engine power: if you have, say, a 40-horsepower engine but the boat needs only 30, you must check the speed at which this power is developed on the engine power curve and calculate on this basis.

Transmission Ratio

Now we must decide on the transmission drive ratio, which means for a conventional system whether to use a direct drive gearbox or to incorporate reduction gear. A fast-planing hull generally calls for direct drive, a semi-planing type 1.5:1 to 2:1 and displacement craft 2:1 to 5:1, but the size and weight of the boat, whether single or twin engines are fitted, and the engine power and speed are all deciding factors. When it is not possible to make a clear-cut decision or to refer to similar boats with the same engine, alternative propeller calculations may be necessary, weighing the advantages of small propeller, low shaft angle, less drag, against large propeller, better manoeuvrability, greater propulsive efficiency.

Propeller Calculation

There are several methods of calculating propellers, from the use of tables and special slide rules to computer programs. One of the most reliable systems involves the use of charts produced from the tank testing of 'model' propellers. These are generally around 20 inches in diameter, although intended as a means of designing propellers up to several feet in diameter. They can be used to provide satisfactory propellers for pleasure craft down to about 10 inches in diameter.

Sets of charts are available for two, three and four blades of varying blade area ratio (BAR). Largely because of differing blade shapes and sections, the results vary slightly from one testing authority to another. However, the propellers you will use will probably have different blade shapes from any of the models, but this will not matter.

The chart in Fig 81, reproduced with kind permission of Netherlands Ship Model Basin, is for three-bladed propellers of 0.5 BAR. The curves are used to calculate diameter and pitch. Efficiency is also indicated.

The first stage is to calculate the 'basic variable' (BP), referred to for three-bladed propellers as BP_3. We need to know the shaft horsepower and speed, also the 'speed of advance' (V_a).

$$BP = \frac{shp \times shaft\ rev\ per\ min}{V_a^{2.5}}$$

'Speed of advance' is the speed of the water entering the propeller. It is almost the same as the boat speed for fast-

141

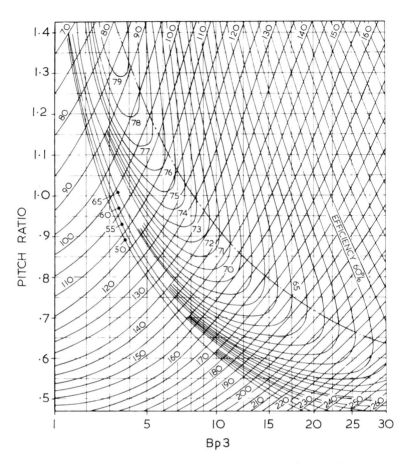

Fig 81 Propeller calculation chart (*Netherlands Ship Model Basin*)

planing craft, but less for slower displacement hulls. Twin propellers being located away from the hull operate in water which is less disturbed and is therefore nearer to the hull speed.

A table of typical factors by which the boat speed can be multiplied to give speed of advance is shown opposite.

It may be stating the obvious to point out that for twin-engined craft the power of one engine is used in the above formula, but the speed of advance is estimated from the combined effect of both engines.

142

Type of craft	Wake factor	
	Single propeller	Twin propeller
Planing sportsboat	0.96	0.98
Semi-planing cruiser, etc.	0.93	0.96
Displacement cruiser, launch	0.88	0.94
Auxiliary yacht, fishing boat	0.80	0.90

So now we use the chart to select diameter and pitch. Having calculated the basic variable (BP$_3$ for a three-bladed propeller) from the formula, run a vertical line from the point on the baseline of the chart to cut the curve of maximum efficiency from where we read off the diameter factor L on the lines going from bottom left to top right. Moving horizontally to the left-hand scale we get the pitch ratio.

This chart gives diameter in feet, so to change our result to inches we use the following formula:

$$\text{Diameter} = \frac{L \times V_a \times 12}{\text{Shaft rev per min}}$$

$$\text{Pitch} = \text{Diameter} \times \text{pitch ratio}$$

Efficiency can also be read off, and it is apparent that this only changes slightly if we move up and down the vertical BP$_3$ line a little. If the propeller diameter comes out slightly too large for the space available we can pick a point a little higher up the BP$_3$ line to give a smaller L and larger pitch ratio. This gives a correspondingly smaller diameter and larger pitch. Don't go too far with this—say 1 inch in twenty inches diameter—it may cause cavitation plus loss of efficiency.

Cavitation

Erosion of the propeller-blade surfaces can lead to blade failure in extreme cases. This will probably be diagnosed by the experts as being caused by cavitation, and it is often due to small propellers running at high speed or propellers with narrow blades and therefore insufficient blade surface area.

If the thrust developed is too great for the blade surface area, small cavities are formed on the blade surface of the back of the blades. Water actually boils in the small cavities because of the low pressure—considerable force is exerted on a very small area as each cavity collapses. The tell-tale small patches of roughness can appear very quickly and rapidly build up to serious proportions.

Badly sited propellers without a smooth flow of water to and from the blades may be affected, even if of adequate blade surface area. If the blade tips are too close to the surface, air may be drawn into the propeller and, as well as causing poor performance of high-speed craft, this can lead to cavitation problems.

It is fairly easy to check whether cavitation is probable or unlikely by working out the thrust per unit area of blade surface and then comparing this value with a graph of safe thrust levels.

propeller thrust =
blade factor $\times$ D^4 $\times$ ($\frac{\text{shaft rev per min}}{100}$)^2 $\times$ P(P + 21) $\times$ S
blade factor = 0.11 for blade area ratio 0.5
D = propeller diameter in feet
P = pitch ratio ($\frac{\text{pitch}}{\text{diameter}}$)
S = slip percentage

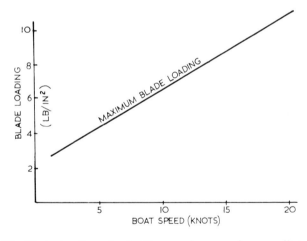

Fig 82 Blade loading chart. The maximum safe propeller load is shown for varying boat speeds

Note from the graph how the acceptable loading is increased at faster boat speeds.

144

Controllable Pitch Propellers

By making the propeller blades pivot in the hub so that the pitch can be varied, the propeller power-absorption characteristics can be varied to match the engine full-load power. By adjusting the blades to a zero pitch position they will 'feather', ie at 90° to the shaft they will assume a 'neutral' position, absorbing no power and developing no thrust. Further movement will bring the blades to a reverse thrust position.

The advantages of being able to adjust the pitch are that you can operate efficiently at the most economic shaft speed, because the engine is always on full load; no reverse gear is required; and adjustment for varying displacement can be made.

Although used to some extent for workboats, the expense makes this arrangement rare in pleasure boats. Also the large hub affects performance on high-speed craft.

7
BOAT TRIALS

Trials and Tribulations

These days 'production' boat trials may consist merely of lowering the finished factory product into a small 'pond', checking for leaks, and giving the engine a short burst in neutral gear. Larger and more expensive custom-built craft may go through the ritual of yard trials, followed by the owner's acceptance trials.

It is the 'one-off' boats that generally give trouble with the engine installation and other mechanical equipment. Production boats usually lose their problems by gradual improvements over a run of boats, so that trials for boat No 100 are more of a quality check than to establish whether suitable pumps, extractor fans, propeller and electronics etc have been specified and installed correctly.

The do-it-yourselfer does not have the advantage of continuity, and may not have had the benefit of experienced boatbuilders and marine electricians in fitting out his craft. He may arrive, therefore, at the time for the launch with feelings of self-doubt, absolute confidence or complete indifference, depending on his psychological make-up or the amount of alcohol imbibed. A common trick is to launch the boat the day before you tell your friends, so that the last-minute embarrassments of changing over battery leads, finding the right oil for the gearbox, etc, not to mention stopping the odd leak, are dispensed with in secrecy, or as near to it as you can get with fifty onlookers proffering unwanted advice.

So the one-off job should follow the practice used with boat No 1 of a new production run—a planned series of checks and tests being followed to ensure that everything functions correctly and will hopefully not give trouble when at sea.

Engine Installation Appraisal

When the engine installation is complete it should be checked over to ensure that the piping, wiring, shaft alignment, soundproofing, etc is correct. The do-it-yourselfer may have to check everything himself, although it is obviously better to get a more experienced opinion if possible.

The production boat builder will call in the engine supplier's installation engineer to check over boat No 1 of a new model. Any serious deviations from the installation drawings will have to be rectified before the installation is 'passed off' and ready for trials.

Running Checks

With the boat in the water and moored up, the engine is started and run with the gearbox in neutral to ensure that the machinery is functional. Operation of the controls, instrumentation, auxiliaries such as bilge pump, sump drain pump, alarm system, radio interference effect, ventilation fans, etc, should all be checked and any problems dealt with before leaving the jetty. A quick burst in ahead and astern will check the functioning of the gearbox, and decide whether you have fitted the correct hand propeller.

At this stage the installation engineer will fit instruments to the engine and in the engine compartment to record temperatures and pressures when the engine is working at full load and speed on trials.

The following are usually recorded:

fresh water temperature in header tank,
lubricating oil temperature in oil filter or at engine inlet,
lubricating oil pressure,
air temperature into engine,
exhaust system back pressure (close to engine manifold),
engine compartment temperature, and
engine revs per minute.

Although some of these parameters will be registered by the instrument panel, more accurate results will be recorded on the special equipment used by the engineer.

When keel cooling is used, the engineer will fit manometers into the system at the engine flow and return connections to measure the resistance in the keel pipes. If the resistance exceeds the engine manufacturer's limit, the water pump will be overloaded, the flow reduced and overheating will occur.

With keel cooling or a DIY heat-exchanger layout it is important to ensure that the fresh-water system can be completely filled. After running the engine for a few minutes remove any convenient plugs from the cylinder head and exhaust manifold, etc where air is likely to be trapped, and check whether the water level falls in the header tank. Top up and ensure that the necessary air-venting plugs are removed whenever the system is filled again.

When filling the sump with lubricating oil to the 'full' dipstick level, note the amount used, run the engine for a few minutes and recheck, noting the extra amount to fill the coolers, filter, etc.

Preliminary Trial

Having ensured that all systems connected with the engine and the domestic and navigational equipment are functioning properly the boat can be taken out on a preliminary trial.

This will be the first time the engine is put on load. Using no more than half throttle the temperature and pressure gauges should be carefully watched. Operation of ahead and astern gears, steering and handling of the boat should be checked. The engine should be revved up and down rapidly to check whether water is thrown out of the header tank. Any problems should be rectified before taking the boat out on its final test.

Speed Trials

Although speed is not so important for a small launch or auxiliary yacht, it should be measured, and will most certainly be recorded by the professional builder on boat No 1.

The technique is to time the boat over a measured distance

in unrestricted water, making several runs in each direction and noting the strength and direction of the wind and tide. It is preferable to do this at various throttle positions as well as flat out, and if you have the time (and patience), a fuel-consumption check is useful, particularly if you are going to make long passages and need to conserve fuel supplies. The fuel-consumption check necessitates a fuel-measuring container in the supply line. This is rather troublesome on a diesel engine, as it will mean bleeding off the low-pressure system. The alternative is to fill the tank beforehand and carefully measure the amount required to replenish after each run.

The economy of a boat engine running at half throttle or below is often commented on. This is due to the power absorption of the propeller being considerably reduced at lower revs, as shown in Fig 83.

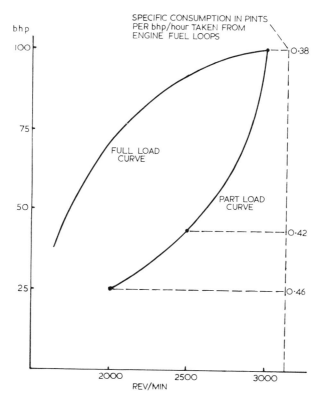

Fig 83 Fuel consumption

149

Fuel consumption = specific consumption × power developed
(gal per hour)

At full throttle = $\dfrac{0.38 \times 100}{8}$ = 4.75 gal per hr
(3000 rev per min)

At 2500 rev per min = $\dfrac{0.42 \times 40}{8}$ = 2.1 gal per hr

At 2000 rev per min = $\dfrac{0.46 \times 25}{8}$ = 1.44 gal per hr

The propeller 'law' curve (Fig 84) is often used to show the power absorbed by the propeller at part throttle.

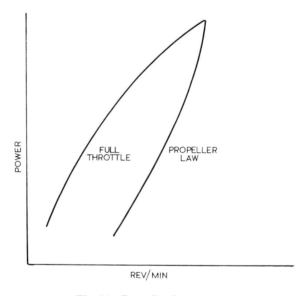

Fig 84   Propeller law curve

The index varies but is often quoted as 2.8 by engine manufacturers. This means that the power at lower revs is proportional to the speed raised to the power 2.8 ie

Power $\propto$ Revs$^{2.8}$ or Power = K Revs$^{2.8}$

A properly matched propeller allows the engine to attain its rated speed or the planned operating speed with about 5 per cent of the power in hand to allow for a fall-off of engine performance or increase in hull resistance. Whether your propeller is satisfactory or not will be checked during the trial runs. In fact, you should record the engine revs as well as the time between marks—you may find a slight reduction in the direction where resistance is greatest.

The reason for this is that the propeller speed is partly dependent on the speed at which water approaches the blades, and if this is reduced the propeller will be slowed up. This is illustrated by the fact that there are propeller law curves for the static and running free conditions.

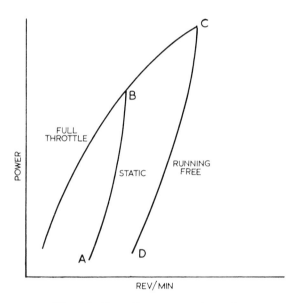

Fig 85 Propeller power absorption

In Fig 85 curve AB represents the boat tied up in clear water with the engine in forward gear at full throttle. With the lines cast off and engine still at full throttle, the boat will accelerate and the governing point B will move along the full throttle curve to point C, at which point the boat will have attained its maximum speed.

Suddenly closing the throttle before the boat loses appreciable way will cause the power absorbed by the propeller to follow the curve CD.

If the average speed of the boat is slightly below its design figure, and the maximum revs are a hundred revs or so below

151

the target a slight reduction in propeller pitch—say 1in—may achieve the desired results.

With fast-planing craft some experimenting with propellers will often increase the speed, even though you are getting a good match with the first one you have tried. A reduction of the diameter by 1in and the same increase in pitch (or vice-versa) may be beneficial.

Getting onto the plane quickly is another consideration, and a change in propellers will sometimes help without noticeably affecting maximum speed. In effect you are increasing the thrust developed, while going from point B to C.

As mentioned in Chapter 6, it is worth taking trouble to achieve a good propeller match; the final choice of propeller may depend on trial and error, but your calculated propeller —especially for fast-planing boats—will be the starting point, and may well prove to be the optimum selection.

Noise

With the propeller finalized you can measure the noise in the cockpit or wheelhouse at the control position with an instrument such as Bruel and Kjaer's, on the dBa scale. If the boat is to be operated in an area where 'sail-by' noise regulations apply, this should be checked at the appropriate distance. Vibration transmitted from the engine and transmission shafting can affect the noise in the boat, and any problem caused by shaft misalignment or the propeller blades running too close to the hull will have to be rectified.

With boat performance satisfactory and all systems functioning correctly, the trials are successfully terminated.

This is the point where the owenr's trials would commence. If we are dealing with a custom-built craft, of course, all the development work to get everything functioning correctly will be for this boat alone, but a production-built craft would (hopefully) have all the snags removed on the prototype.

8

POLLUTION

Boat engines, especially when in poor condition, contribute to the pollution of rivers, canals, lakes and the open sea by the emission of lubricating oil, unburnt fuel and the products of combustion.

Whether inboard or outboard, petrol or diesel, air-cooled or water-cooled, there is a possibility of contaminating the water you are floating on. It does not matter whether the exhaust discharges underwater or vertically into the open air—oil droplets will still find their way to the surface, so in crowded waterways oily patches will be in evidence. Hence the banning of powered craft from reservoirs and other areas where sailing craft or rowboats only are permitted.

The exhaust gases resulting from the combustion system of diesel or petrol engines are mainly insoluble, so that an underwater discharge or a water-injected system contributes very little to the pollution of the water, apart from lubricating oil, fuel or any other solid matter in the exhaust stream.

One engine in poor mechanical condition, so that the exhaust passes a relatively high proportion of lubricating oil, will do more harm than several engines in good condition. Similarly, blocked fuel injectors, incorrectly adjusted carburettors, leaking fuel or oil pipes, discharging breather pipes and the like, will all cause pollution as well as wasting fuel or lubricating oil.

Atmospheric Pollution

Around marinas and crowded harbours, as well as on inland

waterways carrying heavy holiday traffic, the concentration of exhaust fumes discharged into the atmosphere may approach the levels reached on busy roads. Laws have been introduced in many countries of the western world to control atmospheric pollution, because of its possible ill-effects on health, and in an effort to prevent the formation of 'smog'. So far, legislation applies mainly to vehicles on public roads and certain enclosed working areas, but it is expected to spread to tractors and other vehicles used in the open fields, and eventually to control the emission of visible and invisible gases from all internal (or external) combustion engines, which would include boat engines.

Legislative Controls

Atmospheric pollution is controlled in mines and certain enclosed working areas by definition of the maximum permitted concentrations of harmful gases in the atmosphere. In the open air the only legislative possibility is to limit the output from individual engines, or the number of engines permitted to operate. Legislation does not generally differentiate between the various types of engine, although allowance is usually made for different sizes and hence different rates of exhaust gas emission.

As with most things, there is no world-wide agreement on legislative standards for permitted engine-pollution levels. This is partly due to differing political pressures for legislation in various countries, but also to differing opinions on the relative importance of smoke and gaseous emissions, as well as to the differing effects of atmospheric pollution on local atmospheric conditions. In Los Angeles, for example, the high concentration of petrol engine fumes caused smog.

When emissions legislation affects the boating industry, we cannot expect world-wide agreement on limits that would apply, for example, to the marinas around Miami, Florida, in the USA as well as to the inland waterways of the Norfolk Broads in England.

Significantly different standards will mean differences in the engines, and where there are no regulations marine engines will not require the changes to the design or additional equipment described later in this chapter.

Exhaust Analysis

The constituents of engine exhausts with which we are concerned are listed below. Not all of them are controlled by current legislation, as although some are unpleasant they are not generally considered dangerous in the concentrations expected where legislation applies.

Carbon Monoxide (CO) This is the most poisonous gas emitted by an engine. It causes asphyxiation if inhaled in sufficient concentrations.

Carbon Dioxide (CO_2) Although containing the same elements as CO, CO_2 is harmless. It dissolves in water, becoming carbonic acid as used in fizzy drinks.

Oxides of Nitrogen (NO_x) Because there are several different combinations of nitrogen and oxygen, ie NO, NO_2, N_2O, etc, the symbol NO_x is generally applied, although some authorities measure and specify this as NO_2. Some of these gases combine with steam from the exhaust to form nitric acid which is corrosive.

Hydrocarbons (HC) *and Aldehydes* These compounds irritate the eyes and affect the respiratory system, and are largely responsible for the characteristic diesel engine odour.

Sulphur Dioxide (SO_2) Also an irritant, this combines partially with water to form sulphuric acid, which is corrosive.

Smoke Although legislation is concerned currently with the black variety, as emitted by engines needing servicing or in overloaded conditions, it comes in three colours.

Black smoke contains particles of carbon. White smoke is emitted by diesel engines when starting from cold. It is actually a mist of blue–white unburnt fuel droplets, and tends to be worse with low compression–high performance engines. Blue smoke comes from older petrol or diesel engines with worn piston rings causing lubricating oil to burn.

Measurement of Emissions

Gaseous emissions, that is to say the invisible exhaust gases, are measured with sophisticated analytical apparatus while the engine is running on load. A high degree of measuring accuracy is required for tests that determine whether an engine complies with regulations.

Less accurate portable apparatus is useful for tuning engines to determine whether deterioration in emission has taken place while in service.

Exhaust smoke is measured by means of a meter which monitors the 'obscuration' or 'opacity' at the end of the pipe where the exhaust is discharged to the atmosphere. There are several types of meter, among them are the Hartridge used in the UK, the Bosch used in Europe, the French UTAC meter, and the USPHS (United States Public Health Service) smoke meter.

Smoke meters will only work in conjunction with a dry exhaust system. With a water-injected marine exhaust it is necessary to temporarily disconnect the water connection—avoid running the engine long enough to burn the exhaust hose.

The other way of measuring smoke is to rev up the engine to observe the puff of smoke generated. This is known as 'free acceleration' smoke. Because the engine can be checked for free acceleration smoke as installed in the vehicle (or boat) without applying and measuring a load, this method is attractive to various authorities such as the British Department of the Environment, who use it for roadside checks on vehicles. Although it gives some idea of the smokiness of an engine, there is no correlation between steady-state and free acceleration smoke, so that it can never replace the test-bed method of measuring full-load smoke.

Units of Measurement

Gaseous emission levels are measured in several different ways. In each case the engine is made to work to an operating cycle that has a great influence on the emission results obtained. It is therefore necessary to specify the operating cycle. A comparison of results is meaningless unless the same cycle is used in each case.

Results may be expressed as:

parts per million,
litres per hour (or kilogrammes, etc per hour),
grammes per bhp hour, or
grammes per mile or kilometre.

Typical Emission Levels

Some idea of the amount of pollutant emitted by various types of engine can be gained from studying the table below. It indicates the approximate values to be expected from various engines when working to the Californian '13-mode cycle'. This is a typical American vehicle operating test cycle which has 13 'modes', ie speed and load conditions. The units are grammes per horsepower hour, so that, for example, a 100-horsepower petrol engine would produce more than 3kg (6.6lb) weight of carbon monoxide during one hour of operation under the test conditions.

Engine type	CO	NO_x	HC (+ aldehydes)
	Units: Grammes per horsepower hour		
Petrol	Over 30	Over 20	3–9
LPG	Over 30	Over 20	2–3
Direct injection diesel	4–9	7–18	2–4
Indirect injection diesel	2–9	3–7	1–4

The values given in the above table are typical of present-day engines that have not been specially tuned or modified to reduce the emissions.

Minimizing Emissions

There are basically two different methods of dealing with the problem:

1 Cleaning up the exhaust by the use of various devices attached to the engine.
2 Improving the combustion system so that the formation of harmful products is minimized during the combustion process.

Obviously (2) is more desirable than (1), but tends to be a long-term improvement leading to a new generation of petrol- and diesel-engine designs.

We will first look at the 'add-on' method, which was the system adopted on petrol car engines that had to be modified

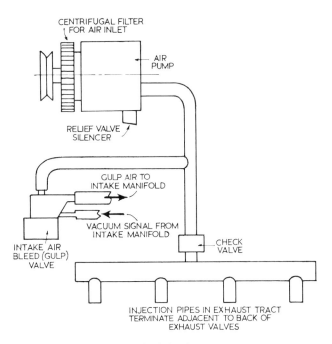

CENTRIFUGAL FILTER
FOR AIR INLET

AIR
PUMP

RELIEF VALVE
SILENCER

GULP AIR TO
INTAKE MANIFOLD

VACUUM SIGNAL FROM
INTAKE MANIFOLD

INTAKE AIR
BLEED (GULP)
VALVE

CHECK
VALVE

INJECTION PIPES IN EXHAUST TRACT
TERMINATE ADJACENT TO BACK OF
EXHAUST VALVES

Fig 86   Air injection system

to meet the first wave of exhaust-emission legislation.

Having made modifications to the carburettor and optimized tuning to minimize emissions, an air pump was provided connected to the exhaust system in the manner shown in Fig 86.

The air pump, which is belt-driven from the crankshaft pulley, introduces pressurized air into the exhaust manifold, enabling the unconsumed exhaust constituents to be burned, and thus reduces the carbon monoxide and hydrocarbon content. A check valve prevents exhaust back flow. The 'gulp' air supply to the intake manifold prevents explosions in the exhaust pipe when the engine is decelerating.

Catalysts

A catalytic exhaust conditioner may be fitted to the exhaust pipe of a petrol or diesel engine to reduce the CO, NO_x and HC emissions. The efficiency depends on the exhaust gas tempera-

158

ture and whether the engine has been fitted with pollution-reducing equipment. To keep the gas temperature as high as possible the device should be fitted close to the exhaust manifold. Part-load running with a low temperature in the exhaust will make the conditioner ineffective.

A sufficiently large conditioner should be chosen to prevent excessive exhaust back pressure and too rapid choking of the catalytic bed.

The Lambda Sond System

This arrangement was developed by Volvo to reduce the emissions from their petrol car engines to meet the 1977 Californian regulations. It operates by controlling the air–fuel ratio, using a sensor located in the exhaust downstream from the manifold. The sensor, which is responsive to oxygen content, is connected to an electronic control unit which in turn operates a vibrating frequency valve in the fuel-injection equipment. This controls the metering of the fuel to the precise amount required under varying load and speed conditions, to minimize emissions caused by poor combustion. Further 'cleaning up' of the exhaust is effected by means of a catalyst in the exhaust pipe.

By maintaining an efficient air–fuel ratio—particularly at part-load conditions—Volvo were able to improve the economy of the engine. Generally it has been found that tuning a car engine for low emissions and using 'add-on' equipment increases fuel consumption.

The same early legislative standards were easier for diesel engines to achieve—particularly the indirect-injection type. Some direct-injection engines were modified slightly by providing special fuel injectors and retarding the injection timing, which has the unfortunate side effect of increasing the smoke level, so that a slight reduction in the amount of fuel injected, and hence the power output, was also necessary.

The introduction of more stringent American regulations and the spread of legislation to Europe, Japan and other countries, coupled with increasing fuel costs and shortages, made it necessary to speed up research into more efficient combustion systems which would reduce emissions without wasting fuel.

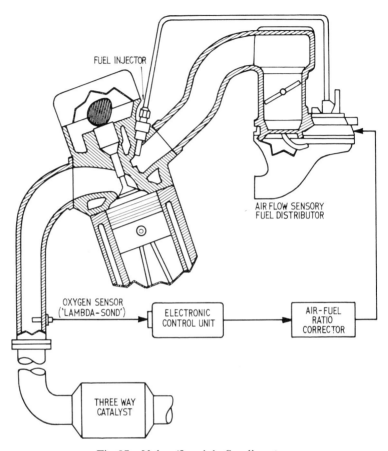

FUEL INJECTOR

AIR FLOW SENSORY
FUEL DISTRIBUTOR

OXYGEN SENSOR
('LAMBDA-SOND')

ELECTRONIC
CONTROL UNIT

AIR-FUEL
RATIO
CORRECTOR

THREE WAY
CATALYST

Fig 87   Volvo 'Lambda-Sond' system

To achieve better combustion of the air–fuel mixture in petrol engines, more effective combustion chambers are being tested, in conjunction with shaped air-inlet ports and more efficient manifolds, to give more equal distribution of the mixture to the cylinders. Repositioned inlet and exhaust valves, four valves per cylinder instead of two, overhead cam-shaft instead of overhead valve arrangement, and many other changes to the cylinder head area, are being painstakingly checked out. This is a very long drawn-out procedure, because one design variation has to be checked against many others, as the apparent advantages sometimes cancel each other out

The ignition system is also very important in the control of emissions. 'Breakerless' transistorized units replace the traditional contact breaker arrangement on many new designs, and the precise control of ignition timing is undergoing research which involves the use of new electronic devices in an attempt to maintain 'tune' over long periods and so avoid the deterioration of emission levels in service.

The sparking plug itself is likely to be replaced by a more efficient 'igniter' capable of dealing with the weak air–fuel mixtures which occur when an engine is adjusted to give low emissions.

Petrol injection systems giving more precise mixture control and more even distribution are already in use on car engines. The higher cost of petrol injection is being weighed against the increased cost of more sophisticated carburettor systems.

Diesel Emissions Improvement

Similar activity is going on in the design offices of the diesel engine builders. The combustion area of the cylinder head has always been the main subject for development, whether this is directed at increasing performance, reducing fuel consumption or minimizing smoke and emissions. Indirect injection systems are generally slightly better than direct ones as far as gaseous emissions are concerned, although not quite so good in the areas of fuel economy and smoke. Much of the early work with varying combustion chambers and inlet-port shapes on engines currently in production was carried out before gaseous emissions were considered important, and in many tests these were not measured. Consequently, some of the old designs are being re-evaluated to assess the effect on emissions.

One of the new combustion chamber designs developed by Perkins (Fig 88), called 'Squish Lip', is a 'bowl-in-piston' arrangement, similar to a direct-injection system but giving improved emissions due to the characteristic of delaying the combustion process, and thereby reducing the rate of heat release, which reduces the cylinder temperature and hence the formation of nitrogen oxides. A spin off from delayed heat release is lower cylinder pressure, which reduces the noise of combustion.

161

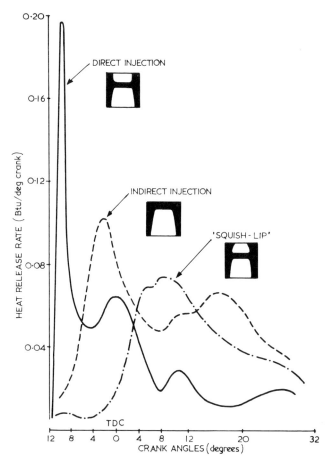

Fig 88 Combustion systems: effect on heat release diagram

More sophisticated diesel fuel-injection equipment is being developed to give extremely accurate shots of fuel to the cylinder combined with injection timing which changes according to the load on the engine as well as its speed.

The new generation of petrol and diesel engines which are evolving to meet stricter emission laws are in some cases existing models capable of accepting new components as described above. Some of the older designs have been retired early in favour of new models capable of accepting the sophisticated equipment needed to achieve the higher combustion efficiency needed.

The next question is how far will these new designs go, and will they meet the higher standards which many experts believe legislation will demand in the future? The legislators are not the only influence on future engine design—fuel shortages and the claims of rivals to the piston engine are causing much speculation about the sort of power plant that will be used in boats during the next twenty years or so. This subject is dealt with in Chapter 9.

Noise Legislation

However, before leaving the subject of pollution I must make reference to the other 'emission' which is only partially concerned with the output from the exhaust system. This is noise, which was the subject of legislation for road vehicles before smoke and gaseous emissions were considered a dangerous hazard. The effect of excessive noise on health has long been recognized, machine operators wear ear protectors and people use noise meters to prove that houses are too close to the motorway, or to decide whether aircraft should be allowed to land or take off.

The question here is whether pleasure craft will be the subject of legislation to limit noise, and the answer is that 'third party' noise regulations are likely to be applied in countries where road-vehicle legislation is in existence. There are, in fact, already several areas where local regulations apply or are in the process of being drawn up. For example, the state legislature of Illinois in the USA has proposed legislation to limit 'third-party' noise on boats built before 1980 to 86 dBa at 50ft. The limit is reduced to 84 dBa for boats built between 1980 and 1983, and 82 dBa for boats manufactured after 1 January 1984.

Fortunately, inboard petrol and diesel engines can be installed with soundproofing to give a low external noise level —some outboards may find it difficult to comply with regulations.

The SAE have published a recommended procedure for measuring the external noise from motor boats under 20m (65ft) in length—SAE J34a. This procedure defines the microphone position as 25m from the boat, whereas different distances are specified by other authorities and boat-testing stations. Noise measurements made at different distances cannot be related to one another, therefore, in order to make meaningful comparisons between boats, a common distance and testing procedure must be adopted across the world. I hope there will be more success in the establishing of a common noise test for boats than there has been in attempts to standardize engine-power reference conditions and emission standards!

9
POWER UNITS OF THE FUTURE

In earlier chapters we looked at the design of present-day boat engines and then considered how pollution is causing changes to land-based engines, which will probably be carried over to the marine versions. In this final chapter we look forward to the next century and speculate on the types of power plant which could be driving the boats of the future.

Reference was made earlier to the derivation of a large proportion of current petrol and diesel engines for boats from automotive engines as used in cars, vans and trucks, etc. Although the number of powered craft, and thus the number of engines for boat installations, is likely to rise in the future, we are unlikely to reach a situation where the numbers would make special designs for boats an economic proposition. In fact, manufacturers who build marine engines as well as automotive and industrial engines generally produce a multi-purpose unit which is designed to be suitable for boats without the design 'lash-ups' of early marinizations. This policy is likely to continue as long as there is a healthy market for boat engines.

Not so many years ago the major criteria for a new engine design would have been: size, power-to-weight ratio, safety, reliability, production costs, and operating costs (not necessarily in this order).

Energy Supplies

Recently environmentalists have made pollution from exhaust fumes and noise one of the most important design considerations. However, an overriding factor is the conservation of dwindling world fuel resources. Fuel economy and the ability to use alternative types of fuel will now come at the top of the engine designers' list of priorities.

The boat engine of the future is likely to be closely allied to the automotive engines of the day, and will obviously have to use whatever fuel is then available. It is therefore pertinent to look at the fuel situation and its likely development.

The crude oil being pumped from beneath the earth and the sea is a fossil fuel which varies somewhat from one area to another. This variation affects the end products of the refining process. The distillation process used is also varied according to the demand for particular fuels.

The following table shows a typical analysis of oil refinery products in the USA, where there is a huge demand for petrol, and the rest of the western world, where fuel oils are in greater demand.

Product	USA (%)	Rest of World (%)
Petrol	45	14
Paraffin and turbine fuel	6	7
Diesel fuel	18	25
Heating oil	16	36
Other products	15	18

Although variations in these percentages are possible it is not feasible, for example, to produce all fuel oil and no petrol. So as long as crude oil is available for use in engines these will have to work on petrol, paraffin and diesel fuel, making the best use of dwindling resources.

Worries about world resources of fossil fuels have led to much activity in the attempt to find alternatives to spin out supplies. Attempts made to restrict usage of oil-based products in cars and other road vehicles by increasing tax and imposing speed limits in the UK, and encouraging smaller-powered cars in the USA, have had little effect on consumption.

Developing countries are carrying out experiments in which vegetable oils and alcohols derived from sugar cane are mixed with diesel and petrol fuels. However, engine manu-

166

facturers are not very happy with some of these blends, which tend to be corrosive and form carbon deposits. A further disadvantage is that the alcohols produced in this way are very expensive.

Coal is another source of petrol and diesel fuels, and was used by the UK and Germany during World War II. South Africa uses fuel derived from coal at the present time. The use of coal is expensive, but its viability depends largely on the cost of producing fuel from dwindling liquid fossil fuels. Improvements in processing coal—particularly the brown variety found in great quantities in several countries—may make it more attractive.

A little petrol is available as a byproduct of the chemical industry, but this is not a significant percentage of requirements and is not likely to increase. Other sources of fuel, such as shale oil, are being investigated, but are not likely to produce supplies of petrol and diesel oil in the quantities needed or at an economic cost.

So how long are our oil resources likely to last? The general consensus of opinion seems to be that if the amount of fuel used for the present generation of petrol and diesel engines remains unchanged, and the annual increase in engine population continues together with a steady shift from petrol to diesel in most sectors, we would run out of supplies somewhere about AD 2000–2030.

But this is not likely to happen. Most experts believe that a different type of engine that is less wasteful of crude oil will go into world-wide use. At the same time developments in the production of mains electricity from tidal energy and nuclear energy, solar heating and better insulation will make it practicable to restrict supplies of liquid fuels to mobile applications, and thereby eke out fossil fuels into the second half of the next century. A further factor in the eking out of crude oil and coal supplies is the beginning of the 'hydrogen economy', described later in this chapter.

Alternative Fuels

What alternative fuels are there that are suitable for mobile use, including boats? Other forms of energy suitable for fuelling internal combustion engines are natural gas, coal gas and

LPG (liquified petroleum gas), ie butane, propane and methane.

LPG is generally 'bottled', and its use necessitates a simple conversion of a standard petrol engine. The 'emissions' from an engine running on LPG are more pleasant, although only slightly less harmful than petrol engine exhaust. The use of LPG for lighting and heating on board is well established, but the demands of the engine would make the storage of sufficient gas impracticable.

Compressed natural gas (CNG) is used on a small scale for industrial engines, fork-lift trucks and small vehicles. It has the same disadvantages for boat use as LPG, and in any case supplies are likely to run out before the end of this century.

It seems very unlikely that nuclear energy could be applied to small boats, and other sophisticated sources of energy like chicken manure will surely never catch on, although the occasional car seems to run happily on the stuff!

Wide Cut Fuels

The specifications of petrol and diesel fuel are closely controlled to suit the performance and durability requirements of modern engines of both types. This limits the amount of petrol or diesel fuel obtainable from a barrel of crude oil. Refineries can extend the proportion of fuels produced by the production of 'wide cut' fuels. This would also apply to the fuel produced from coal.

Stratified Charge Engines

To use such a fuel a different type of engine would be required —similar to a diesel but 'spark-assisted'. Designated 'stratified charge engine' it could use a carburettor or fuel-injection pump, but to secure the best fuel economy the injection pump version would be preferable.

This engine is likely to appear on the scene in the 1990s— first in road vehicles, then in farm machinery, industrial machines and boats. Apart from the additional complication of the ignition equipment, there will be little change externally from the present-day diesel engine. One might think that the rivalry between petrol and diesel engines has at last been resolved by combining the two!

168

The Hydrogen Economy

We have considered the ways in which the types of engines available are likely to be affected while supplies of fossil fuels are available.

But what happens when the fossil fuels finally give out? The disappearance of natural gas and oil will lead to a vastly increased production of electricity throughout the world, partly because there will be a greater need for it as railways are electrified and homes and factories become dependent upon it, and partly because it will become possible to use natural and unlimited resources (sun, tides, wind) to generate it. Once the problems of the safe use of nuclear energy and the safe disposal of its waste products have been overcome it will also be widely used. A surplus of electrical power—particularly during off-peak periods—would enable the electrolysis of water to be carried out, producing hydrogen which can be compressed and used like LPG as a bottled gas. It could also be used to operate engines which would run efficiently on hydrogen—either as a gas or in the form of manufactured hydrocarbons such as methanol. The production of hydrogen by electrolysis will not become economically viable until electrical power is relatively cheap and plentiful, because more energy is required to produce the hydrogen than this gas delivers when used in an engine.

The implications that the production of hydrogen on a large scale would have on the economy are tremendous, with new industries developing to handle the production, distribution and use of hydrogen and allied fuels.

The change from wide-cut fossil fuels which necessitate the introduction of stratified charge engines to hydrogen-based fuels will require change to a type of power plant capable of using the new fuels to better effect than any form of piston engine. The likely contenders are the Stirling engine and an advanced type of gas turbine, using hydrogen fuel in whatever form is most convenient. However before considering these we will briefly look at two other possibilities.

Fuel Cells

New types of storage battery such as the sodium–sulphur type, which has about five times the energy storing capacity of lead–

acid, are being developed. They all require recharging from the mains, however, so that a supply of electrical energy from a fuel cell which is replenished by a supply of fuel is preferable for boats.

Various types of fuel cell are being developed; the methanol/air battery uses about $\frac{3}{4}$lb of fuel per kW hr of electricity produced and so is a potentially viable proposition for small auxiliary yachts. Another cell uses hydrogen–air— the hydrogen can be supplied from a special fuel tank as described on page 175 or produced from a fuel such as paraffin.

Steam

This has been a consistent rival to all other forms of motive power since the early nineteenth century. Advances in technology and the availability of different fuels have brought many design changes which have increased the efficiency of steam engines and made the job of stoking easier, as well as reducing the delay in raising steam. At the present time multicylinder engines which could use hydrogen as a fuel are being developed, but do not seem to have the potential of the Stirling engine or gas turbine.

It seems unlikely that any mobile steam engine—whether of reciprocating or turbine type—can be developed to achieve the efficiency of a diesel or Stirling engine. Although very high efficiency is obtained from steam turbines in power station installations where they operate at a constant speed, the complexity and bulk of auxiliary equipment would preclude such an arrangement in any boat.

Stirling Engines

This was invented in 1816 by Robert Stirling, a Scottish minister, who produced his design at a time when many alternatives to the steam engines of the day were being proposed.

Like several other engines of the nineteenth century, the Stirling was a hot air engine where the heating process takes place outside the cylinders. It is thus described as an 'external' combustion engine, whereas the later Otto and Diesel engines —the forerunners of the present-day petrol and diesel models

170

—are 'internal' combustion types.

Many different forms of Stirling engine have been built, and interest increased during the 1950s when its potential as a quiet, smooth engine with reasonable economy when installed in road vehicles was realized, although not fully achieved until later, when the importance of low emissions was also apparent. Most engines were run on diesel oils, but the design is very suitable for operation on hydrogen and several alternative fuels.

Different configurations of the Stirling engine have been built with inline and vee-cylinders and different systems for connecting the pistons to the drive shaft, as well as double and single acting pistons (as in steam engines).

The Philips company in Holland have been active in developing this engine since 1938. More recently United Stirling (Sweden) AB & Co have been engaged in the development of Stirling engines, and are now concentrating on double-acting models of 'V' or 'U' configuration with connecting rod and cross-head drive, as well as a swash-plate arrangement.

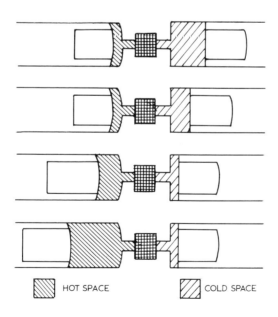

Fig 89 Stirling engine: the four operating phases

171

A Stirling engine works by the compression and expansion of a 'working gas'—usually hydrogen or helium—which is completely enclosed. Heat is supplied continuously and externally, causing the working gas to move continuously backwards and forwards within the 'hot' and 'cold' spaces trapped between the pairs of pistons, and is continuously heated or cooled. A regenerator stores heat when the gas moves from the hot to the cold side and gives off heat when the gas moves in the opposite direction.

Fig 89 illustrates the four phases of the Stirling cycle.

1–2 Compression
The working gas is compressed on the cold side and is cooled at low pressure.

2–3 Displacement
The gas is moved from the cold to the hot side. The regenerator gives off stored heat and pressure increases.

3–4 Expansion
Work is done by expansion of the working gas on the hot side while being heated at high pressure.

4–1 Displacement
The gas moves from the hot to the cold side. Heat is stored in the regenerator. Pressure falls.

In the double-acting Stirling engine the pistons have two functions: they move the working gas between the hot and cold sides and they transmit the power generated to the drive shaft. The pistons are coordinated as shown in the diagram, so that each operates simultaneously in two cycles, the hot upper surface of one being coordinated with the cold undersurface of the next one, so that at least three pistons must work together. Optimum efficiency is obtained by using four or six cylinders arranged either in line, as a vee or coaxially.

Using a liquid fuel, the Stirling engine has a continuously operating fuel injector. Other components include an air preheater, a heater, regenerator and cooler. These items are indicated on the diagrams of the United Stirling double-acting V4 engine and an inline 'U' engine.

172

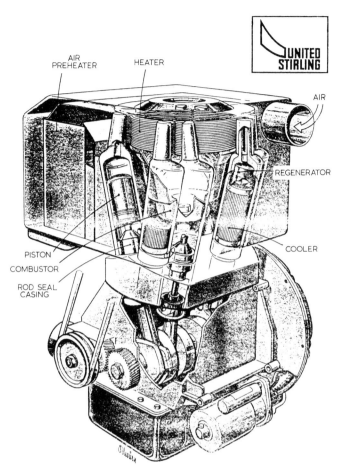

AIR
PREHEATER   HEATER

AIR

REGENERATOR

COOLER

PISTON
COMBUSTOR
ROD SEAL
CASING

UNITED
STIRLING

Fig 90   Stirling double acting V4 engine

One of the problems of the Stirling is that more heat is
passed to the coolant than in a diesel or petrol motor of com-
parable power. This is easily overcome in a marine installation
by the availability of virtually limitless cooling water at low
temperature whereas in a land-based vehicle the capacity of
the radiator limits the amount of coolant available. The lower
coolant temperature also improves the efficiency of the
Stirling engine.

Philips and United Stirling have installed Stirling engines

173

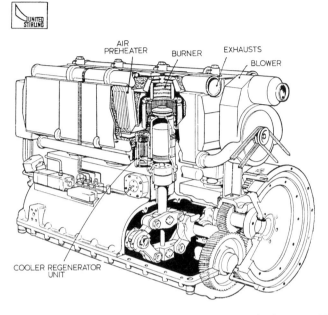

AIR PREHEATER · BURNER · EXHAUSTS · BLOWER

COOLER REGENERATOR UNIT

Fig 91 United Stirling displacer type engine. Nominal power 150kw at 2,400 rev per min

in several boats. A 75kW (100bhp) four-cylinder engine was fitted to a 30ft (9.6m) motor cruiser giving 11 knots at 2200 rev per min and operating very quietly and smoothly with a conventional transmission system. A smaller 7.5kW (10bhp) engine was fitted to a 21ft (6.3m) cruiser with hydrostatic drive to the propeller from the stern-mounted engine giving a speed of 7 knots.

Although great strides are being made with Stirling engine design and development, at the present time there are mechanical and thermal problems which make it less reliable than diesel engines. It is likely to be much more expensive—even when produced in reasonable quantity. The ancillary equipment, coolers, heater, regenerator, etc require more space than equivalent diesel engine components. However, the high-speed diesel engines of today are very different from the models of fifty years ago, so there may very well be considerable changes in the Stirling engine of the future. Continuing development of the engine depends, however, largely on the Stirling's competitors—the main one being the gas turbine engine.

Gas Turbine

This has undergone considerable development, and has recently made great strides largely due to the interest of the automobile industry, which is seeking an alternative to piston engines in order to utilize the fuels of the future.

One way to improve the efficiency of any heat engine is to increase the working temperatures. Ricardo & Co completed a theoretical investigation which concluded that a really competitive automotive-type gas turbine would have to achieve 1550–1600K. This would necessitate very special engine components made from ceramics, because no metals could withstand the high temperature required. Ceramics would be required for rotating and stationary parts.

To obtain optimum economy, especially when operating at part throttle, which is a necessary condition for boat as well as automotive engines, a two-stage compressor with intercoolers between each stage would be needed, so that the resulting turbine would be a three-shaft design. This means that there will be a very compact unit operating at high speed, using expensive materials but capable of using hydrogen in any form as fuel. Like the Stirling engine, the gas turbine will continue to evolve, making use of advances in materials and the brains of the automobile industry, so that in thirty years' time it may well be produced in quantity for cars and trucks, and therefore be available to the boating industry.

Hydrogen Storage

One of the problems in using hydrogen as a fuel is the fire risk. In the USA this has been referred to as the 'Hindenburg Syndrome'—the great airship disasters are still remembered and it is unlikely that storage of hydrogen under pressure in vehicles or boats will be allowed. One way of avoiding the danger is to use a tank filled with absorbent material, such as a metal hydride, which will act like a sponge and soak up the hydrogen keeping it in a safe condition. If the tank is damaged the hydride spills out as a harmless white powder.

To release the hydrogen, heat is applied to the tank by circulating the engine cooling water—this is easily arranged with a marine engine. The tank is replenished by connecting it to a pipe from a bulk hydrogen supply. This takes longer than filling a petrol tank—about an hour—but no doubt further development will speed up the process.

Engines of the Future

The foregoing notes on fuels and the development of prime movers to run on them suggests that inventions dating from the nineteenth century—the Otto (petrol), Diesel and Stirling engines—will continue to develop well into the future. It will be a fight between *internal* and *external* combustion engines with electrical power waiting to do battle with the winner and steam attempting a comeback somewhere along the way. Nuclear energy is the only newcomer to the scene.

The most convenient way of considering the probable development of boat engines up to and beyond the middle of the twenty-first century is to summarize the main points made in this chapter in three sections, each section covering a certain period of time.

UP TO c1990

Petrol and diesel engines will improve in efficiency to meet legislation controlling noise, smoke and gaseous emissions, and in order to reduce fuel consumption. Rising fuel costs and—in some countries—governmental policies aimed at conserving fuel supplies will, towards the end of this period, restrict the larger, powerful boat engines to commercial craft. The disappearance of very large motor yachts will be given added impetus, and the current trend towards more motor-sailers and auxiliary-engined sailboats, with smaller numbers of the larger motor cruisers, will be encouraged.

Rotary engines—in particular the Wankel and gas turbines —will improve in efficiency, taking advantage of ceramics and other new materials and production techniques, although neither is likely to make reciprocating engines redundant during this period.

176

Liquid fossil-fuel shortages will bring still higher costs, making the development of fuel from coal viable in some areas, and encouraging the use of alcohol and other manufactured supplements for petrol and diesel fuels. However, a progressive change-over to wide-cut fuels is likely with the introduction of stratified-charge engines in place of diesel engines and the larger petrol models. Smaller petrol engines will be available for boats as long as they are used in cars and suitable fuel is obtainable.

The development of much-improved electrical storage batteries, and the introduction of fuel cells, is likely to provide competition for the smaller engines up to about 20bhp.

This period will see the beginning of the hydrogen era. The Stirling and gas turbine engines, which are able to run on hydrogen fuel, are likely to take over gradually from the stratified-charge types, although it has yet to be established that it is practicable and safe to have dockside facilities where the tanks can be recharged with hydrogen. The size of the tanks required and time taken to recharge will have to be the subject of considerable development.

AFTER 2050
When fossil fuels finally disappear, the fight will be on between boat engines able to run on hydrogen and those which need the more expensive manufactured fuels. Unless the chemists make a breakthrough by perfecting a method of converting grass or some other unlikely common natural product to a hydrocarbon or other suitable brew, they will have to find a simple and cheap method for processing coal. Although there may be 200 years coal supply at the present rate of usage, it will be greatly in demand even though domestic users at this time will rely on electricity for virtually all their energy needs. So it seems that hydrogen will win the day at least until nuclear energy is brought into a simple, safe and comparatively low-cost state of development.

What lies beyond nuclear energy? The most common patent applications submitted used to be those associated with devices which run for ever without any fuel or energy applied —in other words 'perpetual motion'. When investigated they were all found to be impracticable, the inventor had always forgotten friction or some other factor. The basic principle is that one does not get anything for nothing, and this will surely always apply, although by harnessing the energy of the sun, wind and tides we may get close to this ideal.

Whether nuclear energy proves to be the ultimate or some other way is found of compressing a year's or even a month's energy requirements into a capsule no bigger than a present-day lubricating oil filter canister, the prime mover will be a silent, reversible electric motor with variable torque output as well as variable speed. This will provide an electrical supply to operate the auxiliary equipment, ie winches, pumps, navigational aids, lighting, refrigerator, air-conditioning, etc, which currently require a sizeable generating set for all-electric craft.

While the means of powering boats goes through the phases brought about by technological developments related to changes in available sources of energy, it is assumed that there will be changes in the design of boats during the same period. However, I am not going to try to predict the form these developments will take, or predict whether the fishing boat or cruiser of the future will be a hovercraft, hydrofoil or even an amphibious flying saucer! It is, however, interesting to look back over the means of propulsion which have been intro-duced since the screw propeller was invented in the 1830s. Most of these developments have been concerned with the drive from engine to propeller and, apart from the controllable pitch arrangement which, incidentally, was also invented in the nineteenth century, and improvements in the design of the propeller blades, we have only had the introduction of water jet-propulsion and air screws (as used mainly with hovercraft) in about 150 years of power boating—forgetting paddle steamers.

So will there be further variations in the means of propul-sion during the next 150 years? Alternative means of produc-ing thrust have been suggested, patented and even tried out in boats, including the adaptation of aircraft-type jet engines which are only feasible for very high speeds and involve the expenditure of considerable energy.

If prime movers develop in the way I have suggested, a shaft drive to an immersed propeller with some form of effi-ciency-improving enclosure would seem to be the most likely arrangement. The alternative of highly developed, multi-stage water jet-propulsion systems cannot be ruled out, and I see these two rivals vying with each other for the propulsive equipment business of the future, just as we can expect the various prime movers to fight for the lion's share of the engine market.

Competition can only be healthy and lead to improved designs and a better deal for the customer, whether we are considering the power units of the future or the engine manufacturers' offerings at next year's boat shows!

APPENDICES

1
BOAT SPEED

Equivalent Units

Knots	Miles/hr	Km/hr
5	5.75	9.26
6	6.90	11.11
7	8.05	12.96
8	9.21	14.81
9	10.35	16.67
10	11.51	18.52
11	12.66	20.37
12	13.81	22.22
13	14.96	24.07
14	16.11	25.93
15	17.26	27.78
16	19.10	29.63
17	19.56	31.48
18	20.71	33.34
19	21.86	35.19
20	23.01	37.04
21	24.16	38.89
22	25.31	40.74
23	26.47	42.59
24	27.62	44.45
25	28.77	46.30
26	29.92	48.15
27	31.07	50.00
28	32.22	51.85
29	33.37	53.71
30	34.52	55.56

2
TONNAGE

To avoid misleading data when making boat speed calculations, note that *displacement*, ie the actual weight of the vessel, cannot be derived from any of the following 'tonnages'.

Deadweight The maximum weight of cargo carried. This is generally measured in *long* tons of 2240lb. (1.016 metric tonnes).

Gross Registered Tonnage The total volume of all space within the vessel (1 ton = 100 cubic feet).

Net Registered Tonnage The volume of cargo space. (1 ton = 100 cubic feet).

Thames Measurement An arbitrary comparison of boat sizes based on length (L) and beam (B) only.
(Measurements are given in feet.)
$$TM = \frac{(L–B) \times B \times \frac{1}{2}B}{94}$$

3
METRIC EQUIVALENTS

Volume and Capacity
1 UK gal = 4.5461 litre
1 US gal = 3.7854 litre
1 US quart = 0.9464 litre
1in³ = 16.387cm³
1in³ = 0.0164 litre
1ft³ = 0.0283 metre³

Weights
1oz = 28.352gm
1lb = 0.4536kg
1 short ton (2000lb) = 907kg
1 long ton (2240lb) = 1016kg

Length
1in = 25.4mm
1ft = 0.3048m
1 mile = 1.6093km
1 nautical mile = 1.852km
1 cable = 0.185km
1 fathom = 1.829m

Fuel Consumption
1lb/bhp.h (1.25pt/bhp.h) = 447.387 g/Psh
1lb/bhp.h = 608.277 g/Kwh

ACKNOWLEDGEMENTS

The author gratefully acknowledges the help given by the following companies and authorities in providing illustrations.

Aktiebolaget Volvo Penta
American Bosch, Springfield, Mass, USA
Arona Officine Meccaniche e Fonderie SPA
A. R. S. Marine Ltd
BMW Marine GMBH
E. J. Bowman (Birmingham) Ltd
Carl Hurth Maschinery—und Zahnradfabrik Munchen
C-Power (Marine) Ltd
Cummins Engines Co Ltd, Darlington, England
Detroit Diesel Allison Divn of General Motors Corporation
Dex Marine and Industrial Engines Ltd
Enfield Engines Ltd
Farymann Diesel—Farny & Weidmann GMBH
General Motors Ltd
Holset Engineering Co Ltd
Ingersoll Rand Company
Jabsco Products—ITT Corporation
Lancing Marine
R. A. Lister Marine
Lucas—CAV Ltd
Lucas Marine Ltd
Mercury Marine
Montrose Harbour Authority
Motorfabriken Bukh A/S
Netherlands Ship Model Basin
Perkins Engines Ltd
Robert Bosch GMBH
Saab-Scania AB

Sabre Engines Ltd
Self-changing Gears Ltd
The Ship and Boat Builders National Federation
Synchrostart Products Inc
Teignbridge Engineering Ltd
Tempest Diesels Ltd
United Sterling (Sweden) AB & Co
Warner Gear Divn. of Borg-Warner Corporation
Watermota Ltd

INDEX

189

spare parts, availability, 74
squish, 48; squish lip, 161
startability, 50
starter, 52, *53*, 124; American Bosch
hydraulic, *55;* Bosch, *53;* CAV, *53;*
CAV spring type, *54;* hydraulic, 54;
impulse, 54; Ingersoll Rand air, 55
starting aids, 50; hand, 52
steam, 170
sterndrive, 24, *25;* BMW, *25, 26;* Volvo
Penta, *26, 27*
sterngear, 106-11, *107, 108, 110;*
Teignbridge Engineering, *108*
sterntube, 106
Stirling engine, 169-73, *171;* double-
acting, 172, *173*
stratified charge engine, 169, 177
support, engine, 95
sulphur dioxide, 155
swash plate, 171

tailor-made specification, 74
Tempest diesels, 72
thermal efficiency, 40
Thermostart, CAV, 51, *51*
thermostat, *79*
thermostatic valve, 78
'through-hull' drive, 27, *29*
tidal energy, 167, 178
torque, 62
torsional vibration, 98, 99, *98*
transmission, 17, 22, 24, 72, 76, 93, 94,
95, 98, 99, 140, 174; *see also* gears
trials, boat, 15, 146, 148
trim angle, 13
tube stack, heat exchanger, 78
tuning the induction system, 65
turbocharging, 64, 68; Holset, *64*
twin-engine installation, Ford Sabre in
powerboat, *122; see also 66*
Twin disc clutch, 97; transmission, 93

United Stirling (Sweden), 171, 173;
displacer type engine, *174*
United States Public Health Service, 156;
smokemeter, 156

UTAC smokemeter, 156
Universal coupling, 23, *23*

valve springs, 67
vane pumps, sea-water, 82
vee-drives, 23, *23,* 24, 92; Warner, *24*
ventilation, 117; engine compartment,
117
Vernatherm valve for oil, 91
vessels, commercial, 34
Villiers engines, 72
vibration, 16, 36, 37, 41, 60, 67, 95, 97,
98, 118, 152
vibration, torsional, 98, 99
viscosity of lubricating oil, 50
voltage potential (corrosion), 129, *130*
Volvo Penta engines, 71, 92

Wake factor, 135, 142, 143
Wankel, 58, 59, *59*
warm-up period, 78
warranty, 74
water injection bend, 88, *88*
water jacketed exhaust, 69
water jackets, 76, 78
Watermota engines, 72
water pump, 78; belt-driven, sea-water,
83, 84; centrifugal, 78; fresh-water,
84, *85;* Jabsco, *84*
water pipes, 87, *87*
water trap, 47
waterways, inland, 22, 35, 72
wavemaking resistance, 13
wax capsule (thermostat), 78, 79, *79*
whirling, propeller shafts, 111, 112
wide-cut fuels, 168
wiring diagram, Ford Sabre, *125*
workboats, 52
workboat installation, *120*
Wortham Blake, 72

Yorkshire pipe fittings, 87

ZF transmission, coupling for, 93